HOW TO GIVE AN EFFECTIVE SEMINAR

HOW TO GIVE AN EFFECTIVE SEMINAR

WALTER WATSON
LUIS PARDO
VLADISLAV TOMOVIC

First published 1978 by
General Publishing Co. Limited

Published in 1985 by
Stoddart Publishing Co. Limited
34 Lesmill Road
Toronto, Ontario

Reprinted in 1989 by
Stoddart Publishing Co. Limited

CANADIAN CATALOGUING IN PUBLICATION DATA

Watson, Walter
    How to give an effective seminar

Bibliography: p.
ISBN 0-7737-5066-5

1. Seminars. I. Pardo, Luis. II. Tomovic, Vladislav A.,
1933-   III. Title.

LB2393.5.W38 1989   371.3'7   C89-093246-8

Printed and bound in Canada

Contents

PART II
HOW TO GIVE A SEMINAR

PART III
SEMINAR PARTICIPATION

Note to Instructors

The presentation of a seminar is part of the workload in many courses, regardless of field or level. Not only have seminars traditionally been a major teaching technique in higher education, but with the increasing amount of frustration and alienation students feel in universities because of large, impersonal lectures and isolation from instructors, there is an increasing demand for these small and more personal learning experiences.

Seminars are also increasingly important in government and business. This type of oral presentation and group discussion is being used in a variety of ways, from think-tanks looking for unique solutions to problems, to presentations of new methods, materials, or products.

Seminars are more important than ever, but most students are terrified when a seminar is assigned to them. Many businessmen and government officials also face the task of presenting a seminar with a certain amount of anxiety. The reason for this is twofold: first, the student, businessman, or official may have absolutely no idea of how to go about preparing a seminar. Second, these people may have no idea of how to orally present ideas and the thought of speaking in public produces panic.

This manual is designed to assuage those fears and anxieties. We have prepared a series of simple steps for preparing, presenting, and participating in seminars. These steps include not only how-to information on preparing and presenting a seminar but also a number of helpful hints that will cut down wasted effort and anxiety. This manual may be used in any subject, at any post-secondary level and also by anyone interested in non-academic seminars (business and government).

Picking the wrong topic is a major reason for poor seminars. Chapter one, therefore, starts off with several steps for selecting a seminar topic.

Chapter two presents a set of steps for focusing the topic, thus creating a small, interesting project that can be done in the limited time available.

In Chapter three we give the reader a set of steps for obtaining information on his or her topic. We assume most students will use material from libraries as data. We show students how to use the major resources in the library. For students in seminars who do not use the library (English or philosophy students analyzing, commenting on, or rethinking a philosophy or piece of literature, or science students reporting on laboratory or field research) the instructor will have to provide the instructions for collecting data. This chapter should not be skipped, however, as it has tips on taking notes and evaluating data.

Chapter four wraps up the section on preparing seminars by presenting steps on organizing data so that it is clear and logical, using blackboards, projectors, or handouts and preparing speaking notes and written reports.

Chapter five begins our discussion of public

speaking. Seminars are shown to be a type of small group and the student seminar leader is equated with a temporary group leader. The chapter discusses general tips for leaders, such as behavior and proper physical position in the classroom.

Chapter six gives some specific steps to follow in making an oral presentation: how to stand, use of hands, where to look, speaking voice, and timing sections of the presentation. Throughout chapters four, five, and six we also give various hints for nervous students (i.e. if your hands shake, make sure everything you want to write on the blackboard is done before the class — that way you won't fumble chalk and will write clearly).

We devote chapter seven to a very important but often ignored problem — what to do to get the class talking about the presentation so that it won't fall flat on its face?

Chapter eight is a review of all the steps and hints we have provided. It is constructed in the form of an outline that may be used to plan time efficiently and insure that everything has been covered.

The last chapter does not deal with either preparing or presenting seminars but we feel it is just as important as the rest of the book. In this chapter we give the student a set of steps that allow even the shyest student to develop a system for participating in seminars by asking questions and making comments.

Finally, instructors should note our appendix. To help students in their library work we have included a list of some of the dictionaries, encyclopedias, handbooks, and journal indexes in major academic fields. These titles will give the student an immediate place to start looking for material for their seminar topic.

We believe that with our set of steps and instructions you as an instructor will not have to devote an excessive amount of your limited teaching time showing students how to prepare and present seminars, and the students may relax, present good seminars, and both enjoy and learn from the experience.

Introduction

Webster's Collegiate Dictionary defines a seminar as, "a group of supervised students doing research." But to get to the real heart of the matter, we have to turn to the old newspaper adage, "Who," "When," "Where," "What," "How," and "Why?"

The first three questions are easy. The "who" is you. The "when" is in a few weeks. The "where" is your classroom or office. "What," "how," and "why" are the problem questions. What will happen? You will be expected to find a topic, study it, then teach it to your classmates or associates. How do you possibly do this? This book will give you a step-by-step outline of exactly how you should proceed in deciding on a topic, collecting information, and teaching your classmates. And why have seminars? Throughout the history of education, for thousands of years, this type of education has been found to be one of the best ways to learn.

So what is a seminar? A seminar is quite simply a group of students teaching each other things that interest them. As we have said, seminars are one of the best ways to learn. You always learn more about a subject when you have to teach it.

In seminars you also learn how to collect information, put it together so it makes sense, and then give an oral presentation. It is a set of skills you will need in almost every occupation, from arguing a case in court, presenting a budget, or selling a new line of shoes to a department store buyer, to explaining a new piece of machinery to the men on the assembly line.

In a small seminar group you will discover something about yourself and those around you. Many students believe that they learn only from instructors and textbooks. Seminars teach you an important lesson — that you can learn just as much on your own and from the people around you. If you and the other students in your seminar do your jobs you will find that seminars can be exciting. Not only are you able to look at areas that turn you on but some of the topics that turn on your fellow students may give you new ideas and open up whole new perspectives.

The answer to why have seminars then is that they can teach you a great deal, they have important occupational and social consequences, and they can make the learning process a lot less dull — maybe even fun.

At this point some of you will want to get right into part one and start working on your seminar. However, hold on for another few minutes. Before you start working on your seminar it would be a good idea to find out what goes into making a good seminar. This will help you understand seminars so you are able to do the best job with the least amount of trouble and effort.

So far if you've underlined anything in this book you should have underlined three words — "teach," "information," and "orally." If you want to impress people and demonstrate how in-tellectual you are you may use the more appropriate phrase, "effective communication." That is just what teaching information orally is — trying to effectively communicate something to another person.

Now, what is involved in effective communication? First, you must understand what it is you wish to communicate; know what you're talking about. You have to go out and learn something and learn it well. Second, you have to organize what you have learned so that it makes sense; you must be logical and clear. This step begins with being able to critically evaluate and interpret your information. Then, you must start at the beginning with the simplest facts and background and develop a case from your information that fits together and makes sense. It's a lot like proving a hypothesis or theory in geometry. Third, you must be aware of yourself and your behavior. The way you stand, look at people, move your hands, or pronounce your words all affect how you communicate. There are correct ways and there are incorrect ways to behave. If your behavior is not correct you won't get the message across. Finally, you must be aware of your group. You have to be able to tell when they're interested, bored, or angry and try to control the group so they stay tuned in to you. If they're not tuned in, there's no way you can communicate with them.

These are some of the things that go into effective communication. These rules apply to all types of communication from painting to speaking. We are only interested in oral communication, however, and this adds a nasty little twist. Almost all kinds of communication that require the use of eyes may be repeated. You can reread any piece of written communication, look at pictures, photos, movies or T.V. programs several times. When you are up in front of your seminar giving your oral communication, however, it is a one-shot deal. You have to have all the aspects of effective communication present and working. You must be clear, know what you're talking about, and be able to control yourself and your audience. You have one time and one time only to get your message across. You can't stop and start again or ask the class to come back for a second show.

At this point, we may have you so worried you're ready to drop the course. Don't! Seminars are not easy but there is a series of relatively simple steps you can take to prepare and give a good seminar. If you follow these steps and spend a few hours working, you'll be able to do the job successfully without all the pain and trouble many students experience. We've found that most students, when they know what to do and how to do it, actually have a good time giving seminars and want to do more.

PART I
HOW TO PREPARE
A SEMINAR

1 Selecting a general topic

DOING YOUR OWN THING

You do your best work when you like what you're doing, whether it's playing, studying, or working. You do your best when you are interested and involved. This fact of life leads directly to the first and most important step in preparing a seminar: **Select an interesting topic**. We cannot stress this enough. If you are not interested in your seminar it will be sheer drudgery and you will not do a good job of preparing or presenting your material. In fact, in most cases an instructor can tell a student's final grade merely by the student's initial interest.

Two real experiences may help to illustrate this point. A co-ed enrolled in a sociology course called The Family chose as her topic, "The effects of divorce or separation on female self-esteem." When she was asked why she had chosen this topic she explained, "I guess it was because of my own experience. I have recently separated and I wanted to see how normal my own reactions have been." The more she looked into the topic, the more it intrigued her. She gave an excellent seminar and got an A. A second student was taking an introductory philosophy course and chose as his topic, "The impact of Hegel's dialectic on nineteenth-century European philosophy." When he was asked to explain his choice he said, "I looked over the list and I wasn't very interested in any topic, but I knew we all had to choose one so I thought the one on Hegel might be the easiest." He put off doing any work on the seminar until the day before it was due. Then he dashed into the library, put a few notes together, and gave his seminar. He got an F.

You may be thinking that our examples aren't really fair; one student was free to choose any topic but the other had to pick one from a list. That's no excuse. The philosophy student admitted that all he did was go through the list to find what looked like the easiest topic. Many students make the same mistake. They always look for what they think is an easy topic. If you want the easiest way, you must look for an interesting topic.

The principle step in choosing a seminar topic regardless of whether you are free to choose or must select from a list is to do your own thing! **Use your own life, interests, or hunches as the starting point for selecting a topic.**

HOW TO SELECT A TOPIC FROM AN ASSIGNED LIST

In order to explain the steps for you to follow when your seminar topic has been assigned, let's take a look at our example of Hegel and philosophy. The student took a look at the list of assigned seminar topics handed out in class and immediately began to look for the easiest topic. That is not what you should do. **First, try to figure out exactly what each topic means and what the instructor expects.** For example, look at the topic, "The impact of Hegel's dialectic on nineteenth-century European philosophy," and answer the questions "who?" or "what is?" for each major word in this topic. What is an impact? Who was Hegel? What is dialectic? What was nineteenth-century European philosophy? In other words, first try to figure out what the instructor is asking by defining the terms in the topic using your text or dictionary. If after looking at your text and dictionary you still don't know what the topic is all about, go to your instructor and ask for help. After all, they've also had to attend classes to get to where they are and they've probably been through every problem imaginable more than once. For the most part they should be more than willing to help. But you've got to make the first move.

After going over all the topics assigned to you and figuring out just what is meant by them, sit back and try to begin a process of selection by asking yourself these questions:

1. **Do any of these topics have anything in them that seems to be connected with either my past or present life?**

2. **Do any of these topics relate to what I want to do when I finish school?**

If one of the topics has anything to do with you personally, grab it! You no doubt have heard the phrase, "Relevance in education." It means that something in your education has some personal significance; it's important to you as an individual. If you can find a relevant topic you're in business. But be intelligent about it; don't just rush through the list dismissing topics out of hand. Think about each topic for awhile before deciding to accept or reject it.

But suppose you've gone through the list and nothing seems relevant. Simply go through the list a third time, asking yourself a third question:

3. **Is there something in any of these topics that I recognize, particularly something I like or don't like?**

Looking at the philosophy topics perhaps the word "dialectic" jumps out. Many people have heard that word before when communism is being discussed. Has this topic anything to do with communism? Looking at the second phrase, "nineteenth-century European philosophy," most students would realize that Karl Marx was a nineteenth-century European philosopher. With that, you're off!

But perhaps you're still stuck; you've been through the list and you can't find anything that you think is relevant, relates in some way to what has or is happening to you, or what you want to do in the future, or that you recognize and that turns you on. What do you do? As a last resort, go to your instructor again. Tell him you've been through the list of seminar topics and tried to find a topic that you could get into and do a good job on but that you just couldn't find anything you'd like to do. Professors will buy this, particularly if you show some evidence that you've really tried to understand the topics and to pick one that makes some sense to you. Lists of topics are not usually hard and fast and most instructors are more than willing to help you try and develop a personal topic, particularly when you appear to be genuinely interested in your own education. In most cases you'll leave the office with a topic that both you and your instructor like and a start toward a very good seminar experience. But there is one thing you can do to increase your chances for success: **select a main topic by yourself and go to your instructor with some possible alternatives!**

HOW TO SELECT YOUR OWN TOPIC

Now you're on your own. Either your instructor has not given you a list of topics, or he has and you're having trouble with them; in either case it's up to you to try and find a seminar topic.

Where do you start? Before you can start to get a topic you have to figure out just what the course is all about. What are you going to be studying? **Get a copy of the course outline or description or look at the table of contents of your textbook. Treat it the same way you would a list of seminar topics.**

First, try to define each of the major sections or phrases so that you understand in your own terms exactly what it is you will be studying in the course. Then go to the three questions outlined before: (1) Are any of these topics connected with either my past or present life? (2) Do any of them relate to what I want to do when I finish school? (3) Is there something in any of these topics that I particularly like or don't like?

Now let's look again at the sociology student and her family course. There is not a family textbook on the market that hasn't got something in it on separation and divorce. By looking at the table of contents and asking question number one she was home free with a topic in ten minutes. Better yet, imagine the case of a poor chemistry student who wakes up one fine September morning and finds himself enrolled in an English literature course called, "The sixteenth-century: prose and nondramatic poetry from More to Shakespeare, with special emphasis on the writings of Spenser, Sidney, and Marlowe." That is one hell of a course for a poor chemistry major, particularly when he's just been told that in four weeks he is to give a seminar!

Having read this book, the first thing he does is to get a course outline. He finds that it contains primarily a list of different examples of the writings of sixteenth-century authors. Next, he considers our questions. Number one is a bust: there's absolutely nothing in his past or present life that bears any resemblance to sixteenth-century literature. So he turns to question number two. He thinks he would like to teach high school chemistry when he gets out of school so there's one thing he is aware of — how much chemistry other people know or don't know. His own personal interest becomes his topic: "How much or what kinds of chemistry — or science in general — is mentioned in sixteenth-century literature?" He is now relatively safe. He's got a topic and it's one in which he can do his own thing!

2 Creating a specific topic for your seminar

A NARROW SPECIFIC TOPIC MEANS A BETTER SEMINAR

In chapter one we showed you how to select a general topic for your seminar. There were some good examples of topics given. Why then can't you just go ahead and start to prepare a seminar? If you did, you'd probably wind up with a poor mark and blame us. We deliberately used the phrase "general topic" in chapter one so you wouldn't confuse it with your *final* topic. There's a big difference!

A general topic stakes out an area in which you are interested. But within this area there are literally hundreds of different things you could talk about. If you don't select one very specific thing to discuss you may wind up with as bad a presentation as if you had picked a poor topic and done no work at all. Here are six reasons for creating a narrow topic:

1. With a narrow, specific topic you can deal with your subject in a clear, explicit manner. You will not confuse yourself or your audience. You will be able to present a clear case or argument.

2. You can get into much more detail in your seminar. This will permit you to be less superficial and concentrate on more important material.

3. You will be able to cover all aspects of

your topic without leaving gaps. Gaps can confuse your audience, or worse still give you trouble when your audience asks questions you can't answer.

But before we go any further, let's go back and look at the sociology student again. If she had been in our seminar she'd have had some real problems. The source of her trouble lies in five key words: "effects," "separation," "divorce," "female," and "self-esteem." Let's look at three of them very quickly. First, as she has worded her topic she's going to have to cover the effects of both separation and divorce, two quite different situations. Then she's going to have to deal with self-esteem. We would assume she'll define this as something like self-concept. But from what perspective? There are hundreds of things she could talk about. Finally, what effects will she discuss? Meaningful relationships with males? Other females? Children? Reentering the world of work? With all this to cover she is going to have a rough time trying to be specific and detailed. Not only is she liable to confuse her audience, but she also won't be able to say anything significant about a very important subject. Finally, if she happens to leave out one area — say children — someone in the class is bound to ask about it and she'll be in trouble.

We've saved the best three reasons for last:

4. Your actual seminar presentation will probably average about twenty minutes. You cannot cover a great deal of material in that time and with a large general topic you won't be able to finish. You'll be so rushed and talk so fast that you will be exhausted and your audience will not

have understood a word. A specific, narrow topic will give you enough material to enable you to talk for twenty or thirty minutes in a relaxed manner.

5. You have only a few weeks to prepare your seminar, not all year. In a few weeks you can do only so much work. With a narrow, specific topic you can get all the work done on time.

6. Finally and most importantly, just think about your library. Even in the smallest college library there are hundreds of thousands of books and articles. With a broad general topic the amount of material to look up and read will kill you. You can't deal with the material you will need for a general topic in the time you have. You must have a narrow, specific topic so you can reduce the amount of relevant material needed.

Remember, a narrow topic means you will be able to do a good job on your seminars — and with less work.

HOW TO NARROW AND SPECIFY A TOPIC

We've been pretty hard on our sociology student but you must realize that just starting off correctly is not enough. Let's use her topic again as an example and see just what you do when you want to narrow and specify a topic.

The first step is the same as in selecting a general topic. Try to figure out just what you're talking about. But here, there's a slight twist. Instead of talking about what is meant by the

words and phrases, you should think about how
you'll *use* those words and phrases. **Step number
one is develop working definitions for all major
words and phrases in your general topic.** We'll
start with an example. Our sociology student
uses the word "female" in her general topic
("The effects of divorce or separation on female
self-esteem"). Now I don't think we have to
define the word "female" here. But even if we
did, this would not be a working definition. A
working definition is the types or classes of
females you could use in your topic. A working
definition of "female" defines them in terms of
age (young, middle-aged, old), economic condi-
tion (poor, middle-class, rich), educational status
(college-educated or other), race, ethnicity and
religion (black, white, anglo, east European,
Latin, Jew, Catholic, etc.) or any number of
other categories. *You alone create these categories
and classes in terms of what you want to do with your
topic.* You can't always find these classes and
categories in a dictionary, since they are not
strictly speaking definitions at all. They are your
ideas of what you will look at under the general
word "female." In most cases you do not have to
explain or justify them. Like any investigator you
are carving out one small area to examine. You
state that this is only one small part of a larger
whole. Working definitions are personal classes
and categories that define how you want to deal
with each general aspect of your topic. You do
not have to go into all possible classes and
categories, just those that interest you. *But you
must set up some classes and categories for every major
aspect of your general topic.* You must develop a

framework so you'll know exactly what you're looking for and how you'll use it.

Let's look at a few more examples from our sociology student's topic so you can get a better idea of working definitions. Self-esteem is a difficult concept. The dictionary defines it as self-evaluation in terms of the way others see you; what you think others think of you. The key here is the word "others." What others? A working definition would have to take the word "self-esteem" and classify it in terms of what others you are going to deal with — employers, children, males, females and so forth. You wind up with self-esteem defined in a working definition as the way you think children see you, or the way you think employers see you.

The words "divorce or separation" are easier. All you have to do is define the various classes or types, be it divorce, trial separation, legal separation, the various types of desertion, estrangement or whatever. The word "effects" is more difficult, however. What this means is that divorce and separation will result in something happening to the woman. You may select some changes in behavior that you think seem to be caused by divorce or separation, such as being able to work or having normal relationships with males.

Now that we have working definitions for all major words and phrases, we have some idea of the many things that might be used in discussing our topic. **Step number two is to make columns and list each of these working definitions.**

"The effects of divorce or separation on female self-esteem"

Effects	Divorce/Sep.	Female	Self-esteem
mental stability	divorced	age	(how others
fit into society	deserted	under twenty	see you)
normal relation-	husband	twenty to	others
ship	wife	thirty	males
with men	legal separation	ethnicity/relig.	females
with children	estranged	economic status	children
with women		poor	employers
hold down a job		middle-class	society
		misc.	
		education	
		special training	

Possible working definitions for your topic

Remember, these lists don't have to be complete. All they have to show is what might be used to discuss the topic. You do not have to put down every possible type or interpretation for every major word or phrase in your general topic. But you must put down some — at least two or three.

Pick a word or phrase from each major column above. Pretend you are in a Chinese restaurant and you get one choice from column A, one from column B, and so on. Of course you may choose more than one from each column, but that may make your topic too complex. You may choose from every column, but that may make it too narrow. So use some common sense in your selection. In this case the sociology student should pick her selections based on her own situation, as that is the reason she chose the topic in the first place. She started off with a general topic on the effects of divorce or separation on female self-esteem. Now, let's go through a couple of selections to show you how she could have narrowed this down.

Selection 1: Hold down a job. . .divorced. . .twenty to thirty years old. . .college education. . .mother. . .how her children see her. . .how employers see her.

Possible narrow topic: "How does her perception of the attitudes of her children and her employer affect the ability of a young, well-educated divorced mother to hold a job?"

Selection 2: Normal relationship with men. . .separated. . .under twenty. . .twenty to thirty years old. . .Roman Catholic. . .how society sees her.

Possible narrow topic: "Does her perception of society's attitude toward her help or hamper young separated Roman Catholic women's social relationships with men?"

There are far more combinations available than just these two of course. But this should give you some idea of how to go about selecting your topic.

Now let's take a brief look at the philosophy and English literature seminars to give you a better idea of what we are talking about.

General topic: "The impact of Hegel's dialectic on nineteenth-century European philosopy" (In this case, Karl Marx's.)

Impact	Hegel's dialectic	Marx's philosophy
used	thesis	revolution
same as	antithesis	class
changed	synthesis	capitalism
didn't use		socialism
not the same		dialectical materialism
		manifesto

1. **Possible narrow topic:** "Is Marx's dialectical materialism the same as Hegel's dialectic?"

2. **Possible narrow topic:** "Is Hegel's dialectic (thesis, antithesis, synthesis) used by Marx in discussing revolutions?"

3. **Possible narrow topic:** "If Marx used Hegel's dialectic to develop his philosophy, what are some examples of Marx's thesis, antithesis, and synthesis?"

General topic: "How much or what kind of chemistry or science is mentioned in sixteenth-century literature?"

How much/kind	Chemistry/science	Sixteenth-century lit.
count words	chemistry	Shakespeare
alone	elements, exper.,	sonnets
by type	analyze, synthesize	plays
used by character	science: any word relevant	histories
type of character	to astronomy, biology,	comedies
count words	chemistry, physics,	tragedies
used in type of lit.	geology, math.	Spenser
poetry, play, etc.		poetry
		Sidney
		Marlowe

1. **Possible narrow topic:** "Shakespeare's science: good guy, bad guy, or clown? In Shakespeare's plays what types of characters (hero, villain, clown) use the most words related to science, and therefore, in what manner does Shakespeare portray science and scientists?"

2. **Possible narrow topic:** "Which field of science was most important to Spenser? Are "biology," "chemistry," "physics," etc. words often used in Spenser's ten most important poems?"

Please take a close look at the examples and lists we've just given you. All of them are very personal. They don't even come close to covering all the material within each of the general topics, but that's not the purpose of the lists. Their purpose is to carve out one little area you can handle easily; an area you can get into. Most students undoubtedly have ideas in the back of their minds about their topic, but the trouble is they never get these ideas onto paper. These ideas stay in the background of their thoughts and tend to disorganize their preparation and presentation. Get these ideas out *on paper* and use them to create a topic — a narrow, specific topic that is personal and interesting!

There is one final step in this section on narrow, specific topics. *Always create more than one narrow specific topic.* Some of you may have wondered why we put down two or three different suggestions for narrow topics under each list. The reason for this is very simple: you may not be able to find enough material in your library on some topics. Not all libraries have an equal amount of information on any particular subject. With a narrow, specific topic you will be able to tell in an hour or two what kind of data you can collect on your topic. If you can't, with more than one you've got a backup. Also, some of you will likely discuss your topic with your instructor, and he or she might not like your first topic or feel it's too difficult for you. If you have a second topic, you're in business.

A FINAL WORD ON TOPICS

The process of selecting and narrowing a topic

will help you develop a firm idea of exactly what you wish to do, how you will do it, and why. Also, you will get some idea of the potential for other seminars within your general topic. These two results of this process — what you are going to do and what your area involves — have four important spin-offs:

1. When you begin to collect your data and plan your presentation you will be able to recognize relevant information. Also, you will be better able to organize your material to get your point across. In simple terms you will have a blueprint of your seminar in your mind so you can get the right pieces and put them together properly.

2. Because you know what you're doing, or at least have some rough idea, you will save a lot of time and energy. You won't spend your time running around doing things that are unnecessary, such as taking notes on irrelevant material. Remember, your instructor grades you on the quality of your seminar, not on how many hours you spend in the library!

3. Should a complete disaster befall you — if your instructor doesn't like any of your topics or you can't find anything suitable, you will have some ideas about the broader area of your general topic. You will automatically recognize material you come across in your first library search that is relevant to other possible narrow topics. Therefore, it will be possible to quickly create an entirely new topic consistent with your general idea, and one for which there is material in your library.

4. Most importantly, in narrowing and

specifiying your topic, you have created within yourself some awareness of the relationship of your topic to other issues. This can benefit many students. It teaches you something about the complexity of the many issues surrounding your everyday life. It may also provide you with a number of other seminar topics that interest you and on which you have already done some work. We have known several students who have used the same general topic with different narrow topics in a number of different courses. They quickly became experts in an area and were able to capitalize on this by getting jobs or doing B.A. and M.A. theses. You might seriously consider this as a way of developing yourself for a particular field or specialization.

The entire process of selecting a general topic and narrowing and specifying the final topic should take you one or two hours at most. It does require some thinking but is not really very difficult. Without it, your chances of preparing and presenting a good seminar are zero.

3 Gathering your material

If you are like a lot of students, the minute your
instructor slips and uses words like "research",
"methods," or "data" you panic. These words
make most people think of a genius in a white lab
jacket spending years working over an exotic
array of glass tubes or electrical machinery. The
automatic reaction of many students is to say, "I
can't do that."

But geniuses, labs, and the rest of it are not
what research is all about. Research is just
collecting information. It's as simple as that. Any
information, any time, any place, by anybody.
This information is called data. A research
method is just a set of steps you use to gather
your data. Laboratory experiments are one way
to collect information. Other methods include
field research, going off campus to collect
material, library research, or "self-research"
(collecting data from your own thoughts).

The most common method for students is
library research. They go through books and
articles to find their data: facts that others have
found in labs, the field, or in their own minds.
The second most popular form of student
research is self-research. This method is used in
many English and philosophy seminars. The
student is asked to evaluate, criticize, or rethink

33

some aspect of the thought of a philosopher or writer.

Whether you realize it or not, you have been a researcher and used a research method to collect data many times before. Each time you had to make a decision, write a paper, or give some report, you were doing research. The only difference between you as an unwitting researcher and you as a serious researcher is the realization that you are consciously doing research and collecting your data in an organized way by following a set of rules. Actually, that's all that scientific means — following a set of rules in collecting and using data.

There are different sets of rules for each research method. If we were going to go through all of them this handbook would be hundreds of pages long so we'll stick to library research, since most of you will use this method. If you're using some other method in your seminar, your instructor will give you the set of rules to follow in collecting your data. But if you are employing some other method, don't just skip this chapter. Most of the basic rules in each research method are the same. Also, there are some other topics in this chapter (such as how much data is enough) that are important.

FINDING MATERIAL IN THE LIBRARY

Before you can begin using a method you must find out about the equipment you will have to use; where it is located and how to use it. Many students become members of the lost generation when they begin their research because they do not know in which direction to turn to find their data. No one just walks into a lab and begins to do research. You first must learn about all the equipment in the lab, from test tubes to electron microscopes, where they are and how and when to use them. An anthropologist walking into a remote African village first draws a map of everything in the village, then does a census recording the age, sex, occupation, etc. of every person in that village. Similarly, before critics may comment on works of literature they must know what good literature is. Before you can use your library, you must be familiar with everything it contains.

If you are the average student starting out on your first library research venture, odds are you'll be lost within three minutes of walking into the building. We don't mean just physically lost, but lost period. **Step number one in your research method is to find out exactly what material is located in your library.** Decades ago libraries used to contain only books, but those days are long gone. Now your college library — like most others of its kind — has a huge variety of different materials. Besides books and periodicals (newspapers, magazines and journals published on a periodic basis), your library will probably have most of the following: a specific reference section with dictionaries, encyclopedias, handbooks, guides, indexes and so forth; a record, videotape, or movie section; a documents section, for material ranging from letters to government publications; microfilm and microfiche section; a special interlibrary loan section for borrowing books from other libraries; special services such as photocopying, "talking" books for blind students, and computer search services to look for books; special study rooms and typing facilities; map libraries; and most important of all, many special collections. (A word about special collections. At times various distinguished people donate sets of material to a library, or the library staff may have specific interests in collecting special books on local history or other smaller topics. These collections or books can be a goldmine for seminar research so do yourself a favor and search out material in less-visited areas.)

A final thing to consider is that there is often a number of different libraries on your campus. Different departments and schools may have their own special libraries or collections. You will have to ask at the main library to find out about these small satellite libraries. Don't forget about them. Many a student has been saved by knowing about a satellite library and getting material other students couldn't find or that was not in the main library.

Step number two is to discover exactly where everything is located in your library. Find out everything from where the books are kept and where you check them out to where the reference section is, even where the xerox machines are and how much they cost to use. Knowing your library has material you could use is one thing, but if you don't know where it is you've had it. We don't know of any library that doesn't have regularly scheduled tours. *Find out when your own conducts its tours and take one.* We

have seen students wandering around eight
floors of books for hours looking for foreign
language dictionaries when the books in question were located in the reference section of the
library right next to the main entrance.

After you have found out about the general
areas in your library and where they are located,
you will have to learn where specific books are
located. *Every book in your library will have its own
distinct catalogue code.* There are two basic codes
in the world: the Dewey Decimal System and the
U.S. Library of Congress code. The Dewey
Decimal System gives a particular number to
books dealing with a specific subject. The
number always consists of three digits with two
decimal places (i.e., 633.91), followed by letters
that correspond to the author's last name. The
Library of Congress code is made up of letters
and numbers too, but is much more complicated.
(There are many more categories now than
when Melvil Dewey developed his code.) The
code is made up of two letters, then a set of
numbers. The letters correspond to general
areas. For example, AE is general encyclopedias,
AN is newspapers, JC is political science. The
numbers divide these general areas into more
specific topics. JC–311, for example, denotes
material pertaining to nationalism. All the books
in your library are arranged in order by number.
If you know the code number and the author's
last name, you can locate any book in the library
in a matter of minutes.

**Step number three is to learn all the rules
for using the library and for taking out books.**
Libraries have different sets of rules for using

each of their sections and for taking out books. For example, in some libraries you may go into the stacks and get any book you want yourself; in others you must ask someone on the library staff to get a book for you. In some you may take books out; in other sections you must use them in the library. Not only that, but some parts of the library may be closed to undergraduates but open to graduates. Once you've discovered what material is available, where it is located, and the rules governing the use of the material, you are ready to begin thinking about the material you should gather.

But before we leave this section, those of you who are not using library research as your method please note one thing: so far, all these rules apply to you too! *Regardless of the method you intend to use, you must know what material you may use, where it is located, and how to use it.* It doesn't matter if we're talking about test tubes or electron microscopes, an isolated jungle village somewhere, or your own mind. These rules are common to all the research methods.

WHAT KINDS OF DATA MAY YOU USE?

One of the more difficult problems for students preparing seminars or papers is deciding what material may be used. You have all heard the word "plagiarism" before and nearly everyone has been told in school that copying from someone else's work is cheating. So when a professor tells a student to use material from books and articles many students get confused.

May they copy or not, and how much may they copy without being accused of plagiarism?

When data, ideas, or anything else is published or spoken in public, it becomes public property and you may use it. *You may copy anyone's work, ideas, or data as long as you state specifically that it is not your work and tell your reader whose work it is and where you got it.* Using other people's work and ideas is perfectly alright. It is considered real research because you as a researcher always add your unique twist to other people's work in the way you put it together or in the conclusions you draw.

Plagiarism occurs when you use someone else's work and pretend it is your own. This may be either major plagiarism when you copy an entire paper, or minor plagiarism when you use small passages, ideas, or data without revealing its source. We might also add that the penalties for plagiarism can be very severe. (The word itself comes from the Latin *plagium*, meaning kidnapping.) The professional lives of scientists and scholars are built upon the discovery of *new* data, ideas, and concepts. When someone plagiarizes, not only does he steal the results of years (and sometimes decades) of work, but he also attacks the very heart of serious scholarship.

Always remember to cite data, ideas, or concepts that you have borrowed from some other source. This includes your textbooks and your professor's lectures. If you do that, then you may use any data that is relevant to your problem. Even if you do not copy directly but change the words (or paraphrase), or change the order in a table, or combine tables you still must cite your source.

Your instructor is interested primarily in how you put your data and ideas together and how you use them; that is legitimate research and scholarship.

WHERE TO BEGIN TO GET MATERIAL

At this point you have a good topic, you know something about research and data, you won't get lost in your library, and perhaps most importantly you know what kind of material you need. You're all set to go. There are four very simple steps to follow in getting seminar data from a library. It shouldn't be too surprising to discover that as usual we must start out with definitions.

Step number one is to define your topic in your field's jargon. You have already defined your topic using a dictionary or your text and developed working definitions. You therefore have a good idea of what you will be talking about. But some students do not know the special terms used in their particular fields of study. Nor do they know when words have meanings that are very special in that field. When a chemistry student, for example, uses the word "retort" in an English seminar, does he mean the glass container used in chemistry or the sharp, witty reply? These special words and their meanings are called *jargon*. Every field has its own jargon so that professionals have a shorthand method of talking about very complex ideas. Before you can even begin to look up material for your topic, you must find out the special words that could be used by people talking about your topic. In order to do this you must obtain one of the dictionaries that has been written particularly for your field. Then look up each word in your topic to find out what particular words and phrases this field uses in discussing your topic. If the sociology student looked up self-esteem in the *Modern Dictionary of Sociology* (Theodorson and Theodorson, 1969) she would find not only the word "self-esteem," but also reference to material that discusses "generalized other," "looking-glass self," G.H. Mead's concept of "me," William James' "Empirical Self," "Ideal Self," and role and status. *If you want to get data from a field, you must look for it under the field's jargon.* To find these words, use one of the field's dictionaries. (At the back of this book we have listed some dictionaries for major fields of endeavor.)

Step number two is to get a general overview of your topic. You know what special words and phrases the field uses to discuss your topic; now you should find out some general information about it. For a general overview you should go to the special encyclopedias and handbooks written for the field and look up your topic and the general words and phrases from your dictionary search. This will help you in three ways. First, you will get an idea of what is going on and who the people are who are working in your area. Second, you will get material that will help you prepare your introduction. Third, you will be able to get a good idea of the special subareas relevant to your topic, particularly whether or not there has been any work in your topic's area. This will be your first indication of whether or not you will have trouble finding any material in your library. Remember, we told you that you might have this problem when we gave you the rule about having a backup topic in chapter two. (We have included a list of some encyclopedias and handbooks for many major fields at the back of the book.)

Step number three is to get the very latest research or ideas (in the form of articles) about your topic. Students make a tragic mistake in their research by looking only for books on their topics. If you do this you may be in trouble, first because books are long and complicated. You will have trouble reading them and extracting data in the time you have. Second, books are often several years out of date. Third, it is difficult to find books unless you have a specific author or title. Fourth, every professor has his favorite books and conversely books and authors he cannot stand. It is very easy to get the wrong book and if you do you may be in trouble.

The first thing to look for when preparing a seminar is articles in journals about your topic. Journal articles are short, easy to read, and contain all the information you will need. They are relatively recent in most cases and are usually based on data that is only one or two years old.

But how do you find articles in journals? Look for indexes and abstracts in the reference section of your library. Indexes and abstracts are two different things and they are very important. Every major academic field has a number of indexes. They list every article published in a

group of journals that are relevant to a particular field. The articles are listed not only by
author and title, but in almost all cases they are
grouped by subject. (Not just by general subject
but by key words.) Each author is asked to
provide a series of key words that describe the
subject and content of the article. You may look
up articles by subject, concept, phrase, or what
have you. *An index will list all articles and tell you
where they may be found. Abstracts do this, but in
addition they tell you what the article is about.*

Abstracts are found in many fields. They
publish not only a list of articles broken down in
the same way as the indexes, but in addition
contain a fifty or one-hundred-word description
of the articles so that you know exactly what the
article is about. In only a few hours and by using
various abstracts you can locate all the articles
published in the last three or four years that
discuss your topic in some way.

Following these three rules you can get a list
of all the articles you will need to prepare your
seminar from the reference section in one
afternoon or evening. It's quick, easy, and
painless. (Again, we have provided a list of some
indexes and abstracts in major fields at the back
of the book.)

Now that you have all your articles in front
of you ready to read, what happens if you want
to use a few books? How do you go about
selecting those that are relevant and important?
This is fairly easy. Relevant and important books
are either classics in their field or books in which
authors make important statements that their
colleagues either agree with or dispute. But how

do you find these books and how can you tell
whether or not they contain the necessary
information?

**Step number four is to look at the bibliog-
raphies at the end of the articles you have
found. If a book or author is found in the
bibliographies of more than two articles written
by different people, then you may assume that
it is important.**

If you do select several books for your
seminar material, remember that you do not
have to read the entire book. Only certain
sections of the book will have material you really
need. If it is about your general topic but not
your specific one, you should look at the table of
contents first to find what sections in the book
are relevant to your narrow topic. If there seems
to be no material, look in the introduction. If
both these fail look at the concluding chapter
and index. If the book has anything at all about
your narrow topic, it will be mentioned in the
conclusion or listed in the index.

If the book is about your narrow topic
generally you can read the introduction to get an
outline of the book's material, the first chapter to
get a detailed picture of the author's topic and
research project, and the conclusion to find what
was discovered. The middle chapters are usually
a detailed description of the study itself and the
data. You may skim these for specific bits of data
for your seminar, but most of the "meat" will be
in the first and last chapters.

HOW TO EVALUATE DATA
At this point you should have a list of articles you

want to use for your seminar. If you have used abstracts you have some idea what each article is about. If not, you have a list of articles that sound like they might be relevant. Also, you should have checked to make sure copies of these journals or books are available in your library. Now you are all set to collect your information. But be careful: many students tend to do much more work than is necessary, as strange as this may sound. Do not start taking notes blindly. Too many students do this and wind up spending hours writing six pages of notes about a ten-page article they never use. That is just a waste of time and effort. What should you do to collect information? **Read the article first, including the abstract and footnotes.** Do not take any notes at this point. **Next, evaluate the article; is there material you may use and is it any good?** You must figure out just what you want to use from the article. In most cases you will want to use only a small portion of the article, so why take notes on the whole thing? Also, you do not want to clutter up your notes with data that is not sound. *Take notes only on the material you may use, nothing more.*

Reading and taking notes are fairly straightforward. But evaluating the quality of the article and its data is another matter entirely. After you have read the article you must sit back and think about it. Not every article on your list will have material you want to use. If the article has no material, forget about it. If it does, decide if the data is any good or not. There are usually three explanations for bad data: bias on the part of the author, poor theoretical orientation, and sloppy methods of research and data analysis. Your professor cannot really expect you to be able to evaluate the quality of someone's theory or research methods and statistics, but he can expect you to look for bias on the part of the author.

There are three major clues to author bias. First, does the author seem to have an ax to grind? Is he trying to convince you that something is best? Second, does he present a complete picture or have some aspects of the problem been left out? Finally, what kind of conclusions does the author reach? Is he trying to stretch the data too far? We don't expect you to become expert critics, but you should be able to mention in your seminar that a particular article may be biased. Be careful though; don't attack an author because of his personal politics, religion, or beliefs; attack him for the bias in his data. We'll try to give you some short examples of what we mean.

Sometimes it's very difficult to determine whether an author has an ax to grind. Separating propaganda from fact is a real problem. Your best clue is the use of loaded words. *Good scholars deliberately try to choose words that are neutral.* For example, you may talk about a child of divorced parents as coming from a broken home or a single parent family. Obviously "broken home" makes the reader think only of misfortune. Similarly, the word "discriminate" is loaded, discrimination generally being considered a bad thing. Contrast this with "attitude toward," something that is close to the same as "discriminate" but neutral. If the author of your article seems to be using loaded words, with the result that one aspect of his (and your) topic is made to appear excessively favorable or unfavorable, you may have some bias. Also, be careful of absolute statements like "Divorced women are the victims of discrimination." Scholars don't like absolute statements. They know that the world is too complex to classify things as black or white. If your author oversimplifies what appears to be complex, watch out!

The second problem is that of having a complete picture in mind. You are surrounded by masses of books and articles making sweeping statements using highly biased data. Take the mystery of the Bermuda triangle for example. There is no doubt that planes and ships have disappeared in that area. But do the authors who write about the triangle ever compare the number or percentage of planes and ships lost with the percentage in other areas? No, because losses in the triangle are fewer than in most other areas! Similarly, many young offenders come from single parent families. But does this mean that all children of single parent families will necessarily become involved in crime? What about all the children who lost fathers during the First and Second World Wars? Did they all become criminals? *Make certain the author looks at the case from several angles.* Sometimes this is not possible, but even then, somewhere in the article the author should inform his reader that there are other perspectives to be investigated.

Finally, does the author stretch the data too far? Scholars are very careful not to say too much about their research results. For example, someone studying divorced mothers in Toronto should try to limit his comments to Toronto only. If he does make broader statements from the data, they must by their nature be pretty wishy-washy, such as "the results indicate that a pattern *might* exist in other parts of the country." The author knows the data concerns only one group and/or in one locale so he must limit his arguments to that group or location. Most authors are also careful not to stray far from their topic. For example, research on divorced women in Toronto does not allow the author to comment on the ratification of the E.R.A. in Illinois in 1977. The author is obviously stretching the data too far.

To sum up, after you have read the article, sit back and think about it for fifteen minutes or so. Is there material in it you can use? If so, what is it? Is there any chance that the material is biased? Was the author trying to grind an ax, using incomplete data, or stretching data too far? If the article isn't biased, fine. Use it. Even if it is biased, however, you may want to use it. It may be beneficial to use biased articles to show how incorrect ideas get started or to contrast them with articles biased in the opposite way. They may provide some very interesting points to discuss in your seminar. Either way, at this point you should have noted statements and data in the article that you want to record.

SIMPLE, EASY NOTES

Taking notes can be as easy or as difficult as you care to make it. In our experience most students make it difficult. They do this by simply taking too many notes. Make sure you take only notes you will need, by first reading over and thinking about the article.

The second error students tend to make when taking notes is forgetting *why* they are taking notes in the first place. If you are taking notes as a permanent record and you want the notes to be in a time sequence (lecture notes, for example, where you want to start with the first lecture on the first page and so on), it is normal to take notes on paper in a notebook. But if you are preparing a seminar, taking notes into a book does not make sense. What are those notes for? You are supposed to be taking notes about specific bits of information that you plan to combine with others so you can talk intelligently about a topic. You must be able to combine information. With a notebook, you will have to find them in your notes, then rewrite them in a second set of notes. If you are like most students you won't organize your bits of information just once. You'll go through your seminar pre-sentations two or three times and change them, adding and deleting information. If you're working with pages in a notebook, you're in for a lot of extra work and trouble. Most likely you'll lose something or leave it out.

However, if you use index cards and put each piece of information directly onto the cards, you may easily organize all your informa-tion and reorganize it countless times without ever having to recopy your notes or risk losing or forgetting information. To take notes for your seminar, use the following steps:

Step one: on a master card write the author, title, journal, page, and date of publication. Write a three to five line summary of the article (what it was about, major point, use of data, and if the article was good or not). Now that you have read and thought about the article you should know exactly what specific points or data you want to take notes on.

Examples of master cards*

Brown, Carol A.
    Feldberg, Fox and Kohen, "Divorce, Chance of a
    New Lifetime"
  —*Journal of Social Issues*, 1976, 32, No. 1, 119-33

(Abstract) Cost/benefit of a divorce. Thirty interviews, divorced mothers. Covers economic facts, authority problems, childcare, *social and psychological support.*

LOOKS GOOD!

Myers, L.W.
    "Black women and self-esteem"
  —*Sociological Inquiry*, 1975, vol. 45, No. 2-3, 240-49

(Abstract) 200 interviews assorted ages, education occupation. Analyzed women head of household vs. husband head of house. Self-esteem comes from other black women, *not* employers etc.

VERY INTERESTING FOR TOPIC!

---

*The articles listed on these cards for the topic, "How does the perception of the attitudes of her children and her employer affect the ability of a young, well-educated divorced mother to hold a job?" were found in *Sociological Abstracts*, Vol. 24, 1976, pp. 768 and 1289. The article descriptions were taken from the abstracts of those articles in the same publication.

Step two: for every separate bit of information or data table, make a new card. At the top of the card write the author's name, date of publication, and the page the data came from, then record the information. You may use many cards for a good article and perhaps only two or three for an article that hasn't got much in it. Now you have not only a card that describes the article in general but also one that gives all the information you'll need to find it again or for your bibliography. In addition, you have a card for each piece of information or data. These data cards have the author's name and the date of publication so if the data cards get mixed up you still know what article they are from. If you happen to have two articles with the same date, call one 1977A and the other 1977B.

Examples of note cards*

Brown, C.A. etc., 1976, p. 126

It is socioeconomic *hardships of divorced mothers, not single parent status that results in the negative effects on children.*

GOOD POINT!

Brown, C.A. (etc.), 1976, p. 128

Now (after divorce) have *peace, lack of conflict* with the children. *Have more time for children*

POINT!! AUTHORS SEEM TO SAY FEWER DEMANDS ON WOMAN (I.E. ONLY KIDS NOT HUSBANDS) MEANS DEMANDS SATISFIED BETTER AND LESS PRESSURE ON WOMAN!!! BETTER SELF-ESTEEM TO MEET DEMANDS

---

*The notes above were taken from the Brown article, "Divorce, Chance of a New Lifetime." Students please note that there is only one idea per card, and that each card is headed with the author's name, the date, and the page the note came from.

Now you may combine and rearrange your information to your heart's content and never have to write out another note. As we will mention in chapter four, this is vital when preparing your seminar because you can literally spread out all your material on a large table or on the floor and organize your seminar from beginning to end, arranging the data on different cards in the best order.

There is just one warning: when you take down your notes, be very careful to be as accurate as possible. If you are making a direct quote, make certain that you use quotation marks or write "direct quote" after the passage. Also, make certain you write it down *exactly* as it is written in the article. As you know, if you leave out words or mix up the order of them, sometimes you can completely reverse the meaning of the quote. Also, try to be neat. Notes are no good if you can't read them. In particular, check the accuracy and neatness of data, particularly numbers in tables. Students can get into a lot of trouble if their figures aren't written neatly and they confuse 1, 7, and 9 or get a 6 and a 0 mixed up — or worse, if they misplace a decimal point.

HOW MUCH IS ENOUGH?

We have never handed out a seminar assignment without someone asking how many books and articles he or she should read. Our students usually want a specific limit put on their work. We hate to oblige them because many students may stop when their work is only half finished. In their own minds they have read the limit. We prefer to say do as much as you have to, but many people find this too vague a suggestion. They don't really think they know enough about gathering data and preparing seminars to know when they've finished a project.

If you've done a reasonable job of narrowing your topic you should have a good idea of exactly what you're looking for in the library. If you do, the general rule of thumb for a complete job is to *ask yourself if you have done a good job of explaining or proving your point.* A dozen articles that deal directly with your topic should be enough to give you all the material you need to prove your point. But remember, in explaining a topic you must deal with contrasting points of view. If your first six articles all seem to say the same thing, you should skim through other articles looking for material with a different perspective. If you can't find anything different, fine. You should then look for those that are the most understandable and that use different types of data. For example, if the sociology student finds that all the articles discussing divorced mothers' perceptions of their children's attitudes toward their working reach the same conclusion, then she should look for those that are the clearest or ones that are based on studies of different types of women and children. In other words, if you can't find differences, look for a variety of examples.

If you understand your topic and feel comfortable with what you have done, you have done enough. But once again, if you're one of the many students who worry about not having done enough, *a dozen articles that discuss your topic and present either several different conclusions or are based on a variety of different types of data should be enough.*

This is the end of the third chapter. At this point you have your topic and your data; now it's time to put your information together into a seminar presentation.

4 Preparing your seminar

HOW TO DEVELOP A THEME

Hypothetical situation: you have your material written neatly on all those little cards and you are talking to your seminar group. All of a sudden you begin to realize that something is wrong. Everyone in the class is doodling, sleeping, or just staring into space. No one is listening to you. You have just made another serious error. All that work developing a topic and collecting data has been wasted. Your seminar did not have a game plan or theme.

Many of you will protest that you already have a topic. A topic, however, is not a theme. A topic is an area you are investigating — Shakespeare's scientists, the effects of employers on divorced females' self-esteem, or Marx's dialectic. *A theme is a specific point in a topic you wish to emphasize or teach.* A theme helps you to organize your material. When your material is organized your classmates can understand and follow it. It follows that when students can understand and follow material they won't get bored. Also, when you have a theme you have a reason for being up in front of all those people. You will be working very hard trying to get your points across. This will give you (and therefore, your presentation) a little life. Life in you means life in your audience.

Developing a theme is purely a mental exercise. You must think about what you collected and why you wanted to collect it and then try to develop an approach to it. This is not really as difficult as it sounds, for if you sit down and think you will find rather quickly that there is something that stands out in the material, or that you think is very important for others to know.

But if you become stuck, here are a few steps to help you develop a theme. Look around you and you may notice that people prefer to deal with opposites such as good/bad, or yes/no. They try to categorize everything by pointing out similarities or differences: "Yes, it is like this; no, it is not." *Look for similarities or differences in your material.* Do some authors present different conclusions, have different material, or use different approaches to the topic (have different themes themselves)? For example, you may think Shakespeare treats scientists and science with humor, although he seems to have more respect for biology than chemistry. Or you noticed a change in Shakespeare's attitude over time. Perhaps you noticed that the behavior of some employers has a worse effect on women's self-esteem than the behavior of other employers, or that the effects reported by researchers in the 1970s are different from those reported in the 1960s. These are all examples of similarities or differences in your topic.

Once you have established that the material is the same or that there are differences, you are ready for the next step. *Clarify those similarities or differences.* If all the authors are talking about the same thing, what is their approach and what are their results? If the authors take different approaches and/or have different results, specify what they are. *Do not overlook time and place.* One very interesting theme is always the differences or lack of differences between authors living or writing at different times or from different places (schools or countries).

After you have found some point in your material by looking for differences or similarities, *decide whether you want to just describe the categories or whether you think one category is more important, better, more morally correct (etc.) than the other(s) and should be defended.* It doesn't matter whether you have one category or five; you may either describe or argue. If all the material says the same thing, you may describe the position, or if you can get appropriate proof (loaded words, etc.) attack the single approach. You may disagree with the material and present an alternative that should be looked into, even if no one has done so yet. On the other hand, if you have several different types of researchers who are fighting with each other you do not have to join the argument yourself. You may just describe each position without trying to defend or attack any of them.

HOW TO ORGANIZE YOUR PRESENTATION

After you have developed a theme or themes and a way to approach them you must use them to organize your material so your audience can understand what it is you are trying to teach. **To organize your material you must be logical, coherent, and understandable.** Logical means that you will create a plan or an organizational structure made up of sensible steps, steps that are clear and that proceed from point A to point B. Coherent does not mean understandable. Coherent means that all parts of the plan or organization are related to each other. You have not gotten off the topic — a very common problem with students. Understandable means that you should use words and concepts that your audience is familiar with or that you have clearly explained.

This is not the place for a long and serious discussion on logic, although it is something students should be familiar with. Logic is an extremely large and complex area of study. Philosophers, mathematicians, and a variety of others concerned with understanding how we explain or prove something are engaged in the study of logic. These men study how you may combine certain statements and then deduce conclusions based on these statements. You may have heard of the word "syllogism." This is a type of argument in which you combine two statements and logically deduce a conclusion. For example (1) All men are mortal. (2) Socrates is a man. (3) Therefore, Socrates is mortal. If we had said (3) Therefore, Socrates is a good man, we would have made an illogical or invalid conclusion. This is because nothing in (1) or (2) mentions "good man." In effect we pulled that phrase out of thin air.

No one expects you to use pure logic in organizing your seminar, but you must use two of the simpler aspects of logic if you are to present a decent seminar. *First, you must present your material in an organized manner.* You must go logically from A to B to C. *Second, your conclusions*

must be supported or proved by your data. It is astounding how many students do not have any logical order in their seminar presentations and somehow reach conclusions that have nothing to do with the material presented.

Being organized is perhaps the most important of these two aspects. If you do not have an organized presentation you cannot have a good one. A logical organization may be very simple. For some students all they need to remember is to start at the beginning. Logically organized seminars will have *four parts:*

1. **Your problem statement consists of a brief description of your topic and an introduction to your seminar.** You begin with a detailed definition of your topic and describe why you selected it. This is so everyone will understand your own interests; in effect, be on your wavelength. Next, you might wish to indicate briefly why you think your topic is important. (This is optional and you might wish to skip it.) Next, tell your audience exactly what your theme is and how you intend to approach it (description or argument?). If you intend to argue a point, you must tell your audience exactly what it is you wish to prove. This may be called your hypothesis. Now tell them exactly how you plan to present your material. This is much like our note to instructors in which we told them exactly what would be covered in each of the chapters of this book. Your problem statement tells the audience exactly what it is you intend doing and how you intend doing it. This is the foundation of your presentation. If you do not introduce a

subject or idea here, you may not discuss it in your subsequent presentation, except as an afterthought at the very end of your seminar. This is the first step in being logical, laying out the steps by which you plan to deal with the subject. Remember though that after you establish your plans you cannot change them.

In a formal research seminar the next step would be to describe exactly how you set about collecting your data. This is not necessary for most of you, unless you are reporting on a laboratory or field research project.

2. **The second part of your logical organization is the presentation of your data.** Here you must develop an organization within an organization. Never present a set of facts or figures orally without a very clearly understood organization. No one can possibly follow recitation of a long string of numbers or facts. Your audience will be bored in thirty seconds.

You must decide two things. *First, in what order will you present your articles.* In an argument it is a good idea to start with the people you disagree with first. Be fair; present the best possible case for their side. Then present all the facts that support your point, shooting down the opposition. Remember, what is talked about last is remembered best. If you have different types of articles you intend to describe, decide what types should go first, and so on. If you have only one type to describe, decide which articles you want to mention first and which last. Remember, conclude with the articles you think are most important.

Second, you must decide on a specific order for talking about the material in each article. You must decide exactly what you want to say — what information you want to mention from each article. *You must talk about only the same things from each article.* Suppose the sociology student has six articles, each of which contains a number of facts on the effect employers have on female self-esteem. One is on female bosses, another on male bosses, a third about government, a fourth private business, a fifth, small business, and a sixth, multinational corporations. Combining the articles is not sufficient; each is different. **To be logical you must talk only about identical things. If you do not talk about the same things you cannot compare or contrast them (show differences or similarities).** For example, the sociology student may decide to deal with specific boss behavior (criticism) and its effects, or data that deals with how women interpret the boss's behavior (just friendliness, or a pass?), or take an effect (such as poor self-esteem) and discuss all behaviors that result in this, regardless of boss or job. You must decide exactly what information you will discuss.

Discuss the same data from each article in the same order. In other words, even though the articles may not talk about your data in the same order, you must decide to talk about A, B, C, and D and then get that information from each article and discuss it in the same order for every article. To be even more certain that your seminar group will pay attention and understand what you are doing, you should provide some visual aids during this presentation. We will tell you exactly how to do this later on in the chapter.

Finally, when you present your data just present the facts, never make comments. This is difficult. But remember, if you want to have your audience follow your argument or explanation you must give them all the facts *first*. Then show them how to put the facts together.

3. **The third part of your organization plan is to explain your data.** After all the facts are out where everyone in the seminar can see them, begin to explain these facts. Explain them in the order you talked about them in your data section. Explain A for all the articles, then B, C, and D. Do not explain your data in order of the articles. Where you found the data is irrelevant. At this point you are interested only in the facts you can collect from the articles and what these facts reveal. *In this section do not make evaluative statements (i.e. say something is good or bad).* Talk only about general patterns. For example, if all the articles contained the same points, say so, or if one group left out a point while the other group included it, mention that. You have the data on the table and all you want to do is show your audience the major points they should examine by summarizing the data and showing the general patterns.

4. **In the fourth part of your presentation you hit your seminar group with your opinions and conclusions.** This is the last section of your presentation and here you should say something like, "I wanted to look at X; I found data that indicated the following things —— (this is a

summary of your third section); therefore, with this data it is only possible to conclude that Y is true." (If you are describing here, put all the patterns from section three into a complete picture of the situation.) *This is where you may make your own personal feelings known.* Both the data and discussion sections were concerned with facts only, not with your opinions. Here you may present your opinion using the facts from sections two and three to prove your points. Don't forget that your points in this section must have data from sections two and three to back them up. Remember the syllogism: do not pull something out of thin air. At the very end of this section you may make personal statements that are not supported by sections two and three. These should be put in terms of what future research you should investigate, or what you would like to investigate in your next seminar.

If you follow these hints for a four-section presentation you will have one half of a logical presentation. We have found that many students complete these four sections but make incoherent presentations that tend to get off the topic. You must be careful in planning and preparing your presentation that you do exactly what you say you are going to do. You must never discuss material that is not relevant to your topic and theme, regardless of how interesting it is. This is why we were so insistent in the first few chapters that you get a narrow topic, one you can remember and follow.

If you are organized, logical, and coherent you will have in most cases a good presentation — if you remember one final thing. **In order for**

your audience to know what you are doing they must be able to understand you. When you were beginning to collect your material we pointed out that many fields have a jargon. You will find yourself using a lot of jargon after you have spent some time looking into a topic. Always use simple direct language in your presentation. You should do this for two reasons. First, use words your audience understands or they will turn off to you. Second, very few students have the kind of knowledge about jargon that would permit them to use it correctly. They often try to use jargon and end up making fools of themselves. Even if you've spent a few weeks reading articles, you don't know enough yet to use the jargon properly. You can't speak a foreign language properly after two weeks of part-time study. When you *must* use jargon, explain it carefully. Do not assume everyone in your seminar knows what you mean by "social mobility," "anomie," "paranoia," "self-esteem," "dialectic," "retorts," "reactions," or "materialism." If you must use words like these, explain them using simple, direct language.

At this point, if you have followed our manual, you have a reasonably good topic, gathered your data properly, and planned a presentation that is logical, coherent, and understandable. Now you are over the basic hard work. Next, we're going to show you how you can polish and refine your presentation so that it is interesting as well as informative.

HOW TO LIVEN UP YOUR PRESENTATION WITH VISUAL AIDS

Even with the best preparation it is still possible for a seminar presentation to flop. Your overall purpose is to teach something to your classmates. If they are not interested in what you are teaching, your seminar will not be successful, regardless of the amount of work. People are interested in something when they care about it and they care when they feel some personal connection. The amount of interest or involvement on the part of your audience may be influenced in two ways: first is the quality and amount of interaction between the speaker and listener (in simple terms, the manner in which you make your oral presentation). This will be the topic of the next chapter. The second way to create interest is to remove all potential barriers or distractions to communication. Make it easy for your classmates to understand what it is you are trying to teach. This is something that may be done when preparing the seminar. A major reason for being logical, coherent, and understandable is that the audience can understand and evaluate your presentation. But this is not sufficient.

North American culture is literate, not oral. This is a very important point. Oral peoples typically memorize vast amounts of material after hearing it, remembering and reciting it perfectly for most of their lives. When a culture becomes literate and begins to write things down, this mental ability to organize and remember oral messages is restricted. Literate peoples stress organizing facts through written notes and remembering what is read, not heard. Oral messages become short term, the "here and now" of experience. If we must remember an oral message for any length of time we write it down.

What this is all leading to is that your classmates will have some trouble organizing your oral communications so that they can follow your arguments and remember what they have been told. *The only way they can follow your data is by writing it all down.* However, most students when they take notes do not concentrate on what the speaker is trying to say. They can't see the forest for the trees. They concentrate on copying specific words and never really get the message.

How do you tackle these two problems? **Write the material down for your classmates by using visual aids.** Your audience is literate and depends on written material. When you provide visual or written material for them, they can follow what you are doing and can concentrate on you — not on their notes.

Visual aids are very important if you want to make it easy for your seminar group to become involved in what you are teaching. There is absolutely no seminar that will not be improved by the proper use of visual aids. Remember though that you do not necessarily want to use visual aids for your entire presentation. If your audience spends all its time reading or looking they cannot interact with you and a major factor in gaining their interest will have been lost. Therefore, use visual aids for two reasons: first, to provide some structure or organization for your fellow students; second, to illustrate complicated or detailed material (such as how self-esteem and children are related) or perhaps tables of numbers, or graphs.

The best way to provide structure for your seminar group is to give the group an outline of what you plan to cover. *Write down in simple outline form the major points you wish to discuss in your problem, date, discussion, and conclusion sections.* With this road map to your presentation your classmates can easily follow the points you are trying to make and can see how you are putting things together. Because they are trying to follow exactly what you are doing they should become more involved.

The best way to illustrate complicated or detailed material is through a display. A display is a general word denoting different types of pictures; it may be a chart, a table of numbers, or a diagram showing how various things are related. If you prepare outlines and visual displays the major roadblocks to understanding will be removed. Your classmates can not only handle the oral messages you will be giving them, but they will also be involved because they can understand what you are trying to do.

A basic principle you must remember when you are dealing with visual and/or audiovisual aids is that the more complex the message you wish to communicate, the more complex the type of aid you will need. The most complex audiovisual aid you could use would be a so-called multimedia presentation, which involves sight and sound and the use of a number of different types of equipment. These displays are used to try and communicate very complex messages, such as concepts and feelings. **If the message you wish to communicate is so complex that you must use an aid more complex than a slide projector** (that is, requiring sound equipment or producing moving images, movies, or T.V.) **then something is wrong with your topic.** It is either too large or too complex. You are heading for trouble and you had better see your instructor. *Your aids must be simple to make, simple for you and your classmates to use, and must contain only simple messages.* With this emphasis upon simplicity there are a variety of different aids you may use.

Blackboards are perhaps the simplest classroom visual aid. There are, however, two major drawbacks to using a blackboard: when you write on the board you must turn away from your audience, cutting them out of your presentation; you must also stop your presentation while you are placing your material on the board. This leaves several minutes of dead air in the middle of your presentation and this will turn your audience off. In addition, using blackboards also requires that students take notes. Granted, they have a much easier time, but they are still writing and not following your talk. Therefore, to use a blackboard correctly write down all the material *before* your seminar and never during the presentation. Then you may simply refer to the material. Students tend to copy material on the board into their notes as soon as they get into the classroom and most of their writing is done before you really get into your presentation. If you are nervous and try to write on the board while you are talking, you run an excellent chance of (A) writing poorly (B) dropping the chalk (C) writing down the wrong thing or (D) making a number of other mistakes. This will make you even more nervous and ruin your presentation. You may use the blackboard for both your outline and for any data or illustrations. **At the very minimum you should plan to write an outline of your presentation and all data (number) tables on the blackboard before you begin your seminar.**

Posters are a good substitute for blackboards. Use them if your seminar meets in a room without blackboards, or if you are scheduled to give your presentation immediately after someone else or another class and you don't have time to get material written on a blackboard. It is possible to buy large sheets of paper or poster board and write the material on them the night before your seminar presentation. Use them in place of a blackboard. The weak and strong points are the same as the blackboard, with the additional advantage that you can prepare these well ahead of time, and can use them in a number of different types of places.

Overhead projectors are blackboards without the major drawbacks of blackboards. Through the use of lights and a mirror the overhead projector permits you to write on a piece of plastic sheeting in front of you and have the writing projected onto a screen behind you. This means you can write without turning your back on your audience. It also means you can write simple things without stopping your presentation. Take our word for it: it is *very* difficult to write down a great deal of material or illustrate complicated tables or graphs on an overhead projector and talk at the same time. Another problem is being neat.

Get the plastic sheet early and prepare complicated material you want to use ahead of time. You may even have a transparency made of typed or printed material that will allow you to present very detailed information in a neat and easily read manner. This technique combines the use of handmade posters, blackboards, and the ability to write while you talk. However, there are several problems. First, most classrooms do not come equipped with an overhead projector so you will have to arrange for one to be delivered to your classroom at the right time. You will also need a movie screen. Make sure it can be used in your classroom (are there electrical outlets in the right place, can the lights be dimmed and shades drawn, etc.?). The lights must be dimmed in many cases before the projector can be used, which may cause trouble for some people taking notes. You will also need special pens to write on the plastic sheets. Above all, learn beforehand how to operate the projector. It can create more trouble than it prevents. And remember, if you do have transparencies made of complicated material, it may be expensive. Finally, as with all the methods so far mentioned, your audience has to write material down so you are still putting barriers between the students' complete concentration and your presentation.

Handouts are our first choice of visual aids in a student seminar. The student who has an outline, data tables, or charts and diagrams on one or two sheets that can be handed out to each student generally winds up with a very good presentation. A handout does everything a blackboard, poster, or overhead projector can do in terms of presenting students with an outline of the presentation and complicated but easily understood information. It does a good deal more, however. First and most important, it cuts down on note taking so students may concentrate on you and on your presentation. Marginal notes are all that is necessary. Secondly, you don't have to worry about each student being able to see the material. A drawback is that it is not easy to point out specific things in the display. This is more than made up for, however, by the fact that each student has his own personal visual aid and everyone has identical material (no one copies something down incorrectly).

A handout is neither expensive nor difficult to make. It should never be more than two pages if you can avoid it: one page for the outline and another for data or diagrams. On the outline page leave as much unused space as you can so your fellow students have somewhere to take notes. Make your handout by buying one or two ditto masters and running off copies for your seminar group on a ditto machine. Do not confuse the ditto machine with the gestetner process. A gestetner machine requires a complicated stencil that you can make only on typewriters or with special pens. Anyone can use a ditto machine and ditto masters — even kindergarten children. To prepare a master, write down your material with a pen or pencil or type it with any typewriter. Remember to remove the tissue paper between the white master and the colored carbon sheets. Then find a ditto machine and have it run off. Running off thirty copies of two sheets shouldn't cost more than a few cents per page — often less than a dollar for paper and masters.

Slide and opaque projectors have special uses and you will rarely need them. When the material you are presenting is very complex and cannot easily be copied or described (such as a work of art or a complex diagram), you will need a projector. You may use a slide projector only when you have slides already prepared. This is often complicated, expensive, and time consuming. Most often in this situation you will use an opaque projector. It projects pages of books or the surface of any nontransparent material (such as a painting) onto a screen. The problems with these projectors are the same as for overhead projectors: they must be ordered ahead of time; they need special setups and rooms; you must learn how to operate the machine; lights must be dimmed; students have to take notes, etc. If you must use any type of projector, use it as little as possible. The best thing to do is to get a friend to operate it for you while you talk so you will not have to worry about machinery. Contrary to popular student belief, fancy audiovisual aids do not always improve a seminar. Their use may cause too much trouble for the person conducting the seminar, and the audience will be distracted by the equipment.

HOW TO MAKE SPEAKING NOTES

After you have prepared the outline for your seminar and planned your aids you must prepare your speaking notes. There may be a slight problem here, in that some seminar instructors like you to hand in a paper as well as present the material orally. We'll deal with the paper at the end of this section.

Preparing your speaking notes will be the easiest job thus far in your seminar. You have already made an outline of your presentation when you were planning your theme and organizing your four sections. The outline should include all the major points in the order you wish to cover them. *If you do not have an outline of your presentation, make one now.* If you don't really know what an outline should look like, take a look at chapter eight. It is an outline of this book. Your presentation's outline should look the same.

Speaking notes are an expanded version of the outline. How do you expand your presentation's outline? *Just take your outline* of the points you wish to cover *and your detailed note cards and put the two together!* Take each point in your outline and arrange the relevant note cards in the order you want to cover them. The result should be a deck of cards each with a particular point or fact you want to talk about in the order you want to talk about it. You do not have to use all your note cards. Remember, you want to talk about the most important things you found, so use only those note cards that contain the most important items.

For your problem, data explanation, and conclusion you will have to make note cards. This should be easy for the problem section, since you already have the rough notes you used to make your problem. Just take notes from them as if they were in a book or article. For your data explanation and conclusion sections, look at your outline, pretend you are in a lecture listening to yourself, and take notes. Then turn them into note cards. You should be able to do this quite quickly.

You should walk into your seminar presentation with a few sheets of paper that contain outlines and possibly diagrams and charts and a deck of note cards. *Never walk into a seminar with a speech all written out.* If you do, you will immediately turn everyone in the room off and do a poor job in your presentation. But here you may protest by saying look at all the public speakers who write out their speeches ahead of time *in full*! Yes they do, but they also memorize their speeches so that they never have to read them. They use the text only occasionally to check a point. Remember, you may be nervous or even terrified, but if you are to effectively present material to the class you must talk to them — not read at them.

After you have your note cards all made and arranged, go through them and underline the parts you should stress heavily. This will be your clue about when to raise your voice a little for emphasis. Also, if you find you are short for time (and this often happens) then you immediately switch from all your note cards to only those that have underlined material. Talk only about the underlined data; that way you hit the major points without wasting time on less important matters. If you know your material — and you should after all this preparation — then with your selected note cards arranged in proper order you will find it easy to communicate effectively with your audience.

Written seminar reports or papers are sometimes required by instructors. If your instructor requires such a report, draw one up *but never use it for your presentation.* Because you have it doesn't mean you must use it. If you use it you can't avoid reading it to your seminar — and when you do you've had it!

So how do you write a report? Write it from your speech notes. Just arrange all your cards in order and write down on a piece of paper what is contained in the cards. Obviously you will have to make certain corrections in grammar, spelling, punctuation, and so forth and you will have to add words and phrases to connect the ideas on different cards. Remember, there is no difference between your oral speech and your written paper.

At this point your presentation is prepared; you are all set to get up in front of your seminar group and present it. The only thing you have to concern yourself with now is how to make a good oral presentation. That is the next part of this handbook. You are already familiar with two steps: never read a paper, and put a little life into your presentation. We will go through the rest in the next section.

PART II
HOW TO GIVE
A SEMINAR

5   Preparing to speak in public

YOUR AUDIENCE

Ever since the first rotten tomato, audiences have been a problem for public speakers. *Generally speaking, public speakers must know the type of audience they are addressing and adapt their presentation to the interests and temperament of that audience if they want them to listen.* There are two basic adaptations. First, the topic, visual aids, and text must be tailored to the likes and dislikes of the audience. Second, the speaker's behavior (formal, funny, casual, etc.) must be tailored to the behavior the audience expects from a public speaker. In addition, the speaker must exercise control over his audience. In a seminar situation some of these problems disappear. In public speaking generally, the audience and speaker are usually strangers. The audience members have also come for a number of different reasons ranging from just visiting to heckling. On the other hand, a seminar is made up of people who know each other. Speakers and audience members meet and interact with some regularity; a seminar has a specific purpose that is shared by the members. If you use your own judgment about the topic, visual aids, words, etc., you will be fairly close to the likes and dislikes of the rest of the group.

Your major problem in presenting a seminar will be your behavior. The key to an effective presentation lies not in the topic but in how you control your seminar during your presentation. Although you and your seminar may share some common interests and agree on styles of presentation, this is not enough. A speaker must behave like a leader and control his audience. *Effective public speakers are those who lead not by forcing people to do something but by making it easier for the audience to do what it wants to do.* If you know what behaviors are natural for your audience you will be able to tailor your own behavior so that you act like a leader, by facilitating the group's operation, helping it work well together, and achieving its common purpose.

SEMINARS AS SMALL GROUPS

Leading a seminar by facilitating the group's normal behavior is not as difficult as it sounds.

The general public speaker must be able to read an audience's behavior while speaking and make a number of instantaneous decisions. But a seminar leader does not. *By virtue of its continued interaction, size, and common purpose a seminar becomes a special type of group that social scientists call a small group.* Small groups have been studied by social scientists for decades. They have discovered that specific patterns of behavior develop in all small groups. This means that seminar leaders do not have to analyze the situation as it develops. They know what will happen and can sit down and plan everything beforehand.

For this task you need be concerned only with a few small group behaviors so that you can exercise some control over the group for twenty or thirty minutes. You must know some of the major functions needed so that the group may operate efficiently, the types of persons who perform these functions, and the major problems that prevent these functions from being performed.[1] In short, how a group operates.

A small group has three sets of functions: a purpose or task, a mechanism for integrating various parts or persons into the group, and

---

[1] The major concepts and terms used in this section on small groups are taken from the U.S. National Education Association's National Training Laboratories volume, *Group Development* (Benne and Sheats, Washington, 1961). Although we do not necessarily support all of the conclusions in the articles, or the use of T Groups, we have chosen this volume because the articles are among the best known in the field and the concepts and terms need no extensive definition.

means for individuals to gain personal satisfaction. Each of these major functions is taken care of by people performing a set of specific duties and behaviors that social scientists call roles. A single seminar member may have more than one role, so as a seminar leader you must be aware of these major roles and see that they are performed.

The major function of the seminar is learning and you must ensure that this task is accomplished. The following roles are essential to this task:

Initiator-contributor: the person in the group who proposes new ideas

Information giver: presents facts or authoritative generalizations

Opinion giver: states beliefs and opinions, proposes what should become group's view

Coordinator: shows or clarifies the relationships between various ideas

Orienter: defines the position, summarizing what has occurred, raises questions about the direction the group is taking.[2]

The leader should be the intiator, the information and opinion giver. These roles provide all of the new information for the group. The roles of coordinator and orienter may be provided by your instructor. If he or she does not fulfill these functions then you will have

[2] Ibid., pp. 53-5.

to do so in your presentation. In thinking about these roles you may find that some people in your seminar fill them even though they are not presenting a seminar (for example, the person who is always trying to give opinions or more information on the topic). Make a mental note of these people. Two more task-oriented roles are also important:

> *Information seeker:* asks for clarification, more information or facts
>
> *Opinion seeker:* asks for clarification of opinions

Several other roles concerned with the integration of the group and personal satisfaction you are liable to have in your group are noted below. When examining them, try to think of whether or not they describe people in your own seminar:

Integrative roles:

> *Encourager:* praises, agrees with, and accepts the contributions of others, is warm and supportive
>
> *Harmonizer:* mediates the differences between other members, also relieves tension with jokes
>
> *Compromiser:* one of the people in the argument who will usually offer some compromise
>
> *Gatekeeper and expediter:* (very important) attempts to encourage or facilitate the participation of others, or keeps time so all may get their fair share of attention

Personal satisfaction:
> *Aggressor:* expresses disapproval, attacks with cutting jokes, etc.
> *Blocker:* always disagrees or opposes, tries to bring up old issues
> *Recognition seeker:* works in many ways to call attention to self, boasts reports on personal achievements, etc.
> *Dominator:* tries to assert authority or superiority, gives directions authoritatively, asserts superior status, interrupts others to comment
> *Special-interest pleader:* takes up the cause for business, workers, third world, women, etc., and tries to force every topic into these special interests

Seminars and small groups fail for three general reasons, all of them the fault of the seminar leader! First and most important in seminars is *apathy*. That "I don't give a damn" feeling results from a dull, boring seminar. A dull seminar is one in which the audience doesn't participate. Participation can be created by the speaker's behavior.

The second major problem with seminars is that some vital function is not being performed. For example, if there is no gatekeeper those present may never get a chance to ask questions, so apathy sets in. There are a number of other vital functions. Unresolved conflicts will cause people to ignore your presentation as they try to score points on others. Also, the lack of a coordinator or orienter may cause the seminar members to become confused after several different presentations and turn off to the rest of the presentation.

The third major problem in a seminar is the "hidden agenda." This phenomenon appears when you have special-interest pleaders who try to get their own message across regardless of the seminar topic, or when the exact purpose of the seminar is not clear enough and no one knows exactly what to do.

HOW TO BE A LEADER

Here, we are going to discuss some specific items you may plan for so that you may become an effective leader in your seminar presentation. The major consideration in your plan should be that the leader initiates all discussions. You don't have to be an aggressive, noisy, domineering person. That is not the way to lead. Effective leaders help people do what they want to do. **All you have to do is do things first; take the lead.** You must be able to anticipate long-term problems that could arise in your group, as well as develop some involvement in your presentation.

Long-term problems can end your seminar before it begins. The first part of your plan should involve spending a few minutes thinking about past seminars. We told you when we talked about the different roles in groups to think about your group and to see if you could pick out persons who played various roles. With those people in mind, is your seminar an exciting experience, or is there bickering, boredom, people cutting class, etc? If your seminar has some of the latter, try to figure out the reason.

All groups have bad days when there are problems, so don't worry if there are occasional flareups in your seminar. What you should worry about is people constantly fighting or who seem to be turned off. *Long-term problems in your seminar will develop because of a lack of roles or conflict between two roles.* Look for these problems and write them down. Then plan some way to mention them in the first few seconds of your presentation. This is how you start things and take the lead. If the problem is lack of a role (coordinator, gatekeeper, harmonizer, etc.), try to fill that role yourself for the first one or two minutes of your presentation. Is there anyone in the group who tries to resolve conflicts? Has anyone tried to orient and give structure to the group? If the problem is lack of coordination, describe how your presentation fits into the lectures and with other presentations. If your group has an aggressor and a special-interest pleader who have been at each other's throat, start out by acknowledging the conflict in a light way, but get it into the open. For example:

> Jim and Pete have been arguing for the past week over the effects of the system on the factory worker. My presentation will probably add some fuel to that fire as I'm going to talk about Marx and Marx's philosophy. Maybe after my presentation some other people in the class might like to bring up their ideas about how this relates to Jim and Pete's argument and give them a rest today.

If there are no real long-term problems in

the group, your task is to get your audience involved in the presentation. First, you need a list of the personalities in your group. Then in your presentation you must periodically take the role of the gatekeeper, encourager, or har- monizer. Write down and plan on mentioning the names of several group members in your presentation when you are at a point you think might interest or be relevant to them. For example, if two people had a disagreement last seminar and in your presentation you have some material relevant to that disagreement, play the harmonizer or encourager by mentioning that so and so had a great discussion on that point last week and that with this new data the group might be able to continue to try and reach some conclusion after the presentation. By mention- ing these two people in a positive and harmoniz- ing way you automatically have two participants who will hang on your every word for the rest of the presentation. They will also do everything they can to start a discussion after your presenta- tion. Chances are they will not be apathetic.

Don't try to mention everyone in the room; that is not necessary. As soon as a couple of people get excited and involved, everyone else in the room will catch the disease. Take what you think are two, three, or four major things that have happened before, or people who have been central to past seminars as orienters, aggressors, special-interest pleaders, etc., and try and bring them into your presentation. By planning to specifically note problems that have made past presentations bad and people who might contri- bute to your presentation, you will be directly involving other people in your actions. You will be catering to their interests and concerns. You are permitting them to do their own thing and even helping them. But by moving first you are leading and in control!

CREATING A LEADER'S ENVIRONMENT

Planning to be a leader by taking the initiative is only one part of being a leader. In addition to planning how to deal with other people, a leader must also create an environment and behave like a leader. In chapter six we will talk about behaving like a leader. For now, we must talk about creating a leadership environment. Each one of you is aware that space, and how you use it, is a big factor in your status. It is widely believed that the more important an executive is in a company the larger his desk, office, and window space will be and the higher up in the building he will be. The more powerful you are the more space you seem to have.

In a university, undergraduates are lucky to have locker space while graduate students have offices, and assistant, associate, or full professors have different-size offices with or without windows, depending upon their rank.

Leaders have had one rule about space since the beginning of time: **take the high ground!** If you are a leader, you must be in a physical position where you dominate all others. You must take the high ground where you can see everyone else and be seen by them as well. A second thing to remember is to sit where you can

High ground
The leader's space in your seminar

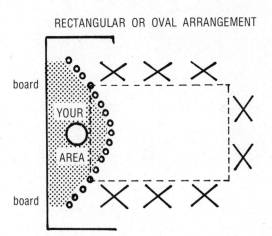

RECTANGULAR OR OVAL ARRANGEMENT

board

YOUR

AREA

board

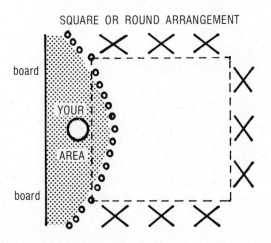

SQUARE OR ROUND ARRANGEMENT

board

YOUR

AREA

board

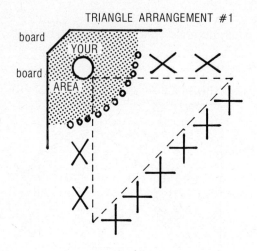

TRIANGLE ARRANGEMENT #1

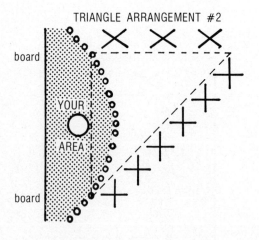

TRIANGLE ARRANGEMENT #2

CLEAR AREAS AND BLACKBOARDS IN STANDARD CLASSROOMS

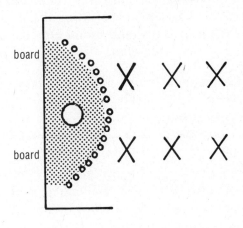

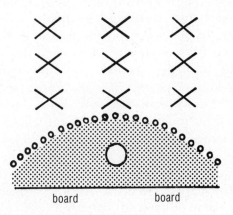

catch the eye of everyone in your group. Around a table this means at the head. If your instructor happens to be sitting there, you may sit at the foot of the table or ask him to move. But never sit with members of your audience.

1. Keep a semicircular area clean in front of you
2. Keep the blackboards and/or projector screens off to one side
3. If possible in your seating arrangement and blackboards, try to face the door

A third point to remember in your leadership environment is whether or not you will be using communication aids. If you are using the blackboard, projectors, or some other aid that has a specific place, your dominant position must be in the right spot to use these fixed aids. You should be in front of the board, poster, or screen, so that when people look at it they must look at you too. Never put yourself in a position where in order to use your aids you must stumble over people or walk around a table or make a movement that may distract your audience. You must be in a position where all you have to do is stand and reach out and your aid is there. If you can't do this, get someone else to operate the aid (i.e. run the projector or hand out the paper). Keep to the high ground and don't come down until you are finished leading. If you have to trot to the back of the room to operate a projector you become just another participant — not a leader!

In order to create this leadership environment you may have to get to the seminar room before everyone else. This is particularly true after the first two weeks of class because people tend to establish their own private seats. You may have to move chairs around and take seats away from people, but don't be afraid to do this. *Remember, you are where you sit!* If you are in a place that physically reflects an elevated status you will be treated with that status. Think of how many times you have heard the phrase "respect for the office". People will respect you and let you lead them if you are in a position they respect.

FINAL PREPARATIONS

The last two things you should do before you get set to get up and talk is to *make a written plan* for your leadership behavior and environment, *and practice your full presentation*, including the plan for involving others, solving problems, and making the environment work for you. We do not want you to spend any more time and effort working than you really have to but these two steps are vital. If you do not have your plans written in front of you, you will forget something. Also, you must practice your speech so you are familiar with what you want to say, how you want to say it, and all the gestures and movements you will want to use.

Write a script or outline for your leadership behavior. Specify exactly the points you must mention, and when you must mention them. This does not mean a speech word for word. The leadership statements should be written on your note cards and put in the appropriate spots. Put all your movements and gestures on note cards too and shuffle them into your notes. We've often seen students forget to go to the board or to the projector simply because they were nervous. If you have it written in your notes you can get up and go to the board and point out the figures for 1975 or whatever. That way you can't forget. Practice your presentation from top to bottom at least twice, the final time being the night before your presentation. Give it the full treatment, regardless of what your roommate says. Practicing does three major things: first, it gives you a chance to learn what you want to say. Second, because you will cover virtually everything in your presentation, from the people you want to mention to the use of aids, you will quickly discover any potential problems you've forgotten about (such as where to plug in the overhead projector, getting someone to operate the lights, etc.). Finally, it clarifies your presentation in your own mind so that you will be able to move and talk from habit, even if you don't know exactly what you're doing.

Some students don't like the idea of practicing. They feel that they don't need it, and besides it's embarrassing to wander around a room talking to the walls, pretending to write on a blackboard or hand out papers. Our reply to this is that professionals — actors, politicians, and people who depend on public appearances for their livelihood — all practice, often for hours. Even if they've given the same speech or played the same part a hundred times, they still practice.

If you have followed our handbook so far

you are all set to get up in front of your seminar.
You have a good topic and appropriate material
complete with aids to explain all your points.
You have thought about your seminar group
and the problems and people in it. You have
planned how you will lead the group by being a
facilitator, helping people do what they want to
do, and by getting them involved in your topic.
You have also planned an environment for
yourself in which you will be the physical leader
by virtue of your place in the room and by the
way you control the space (i.e. having everything
at your fingertips). Finally, you have practiced
and have anticipated any hidden problems in
your presentation. You should now be comfortable with what you want to say and how you want
to say it.

6 Speaking to the class

Public speakers may have great topics, material, and plans and still blow the whole thing the minute they get up to speak. Why? By not *acting* like a leader. We've already told you that the best leader is not the autocratic dictator who gets up before an audience with his chest puffed out strutting back and forth shouting and pounding like a Hitler. *The good leader is someone who starts things happening.* Speaking in front of your class, you don't have to fight, dominate, or force. Just start things happening.

In public speaking you are interacting — exchanging information, facts, opinions, etc. with other people. Now, how do you send signals to other people that you do or don't want to interact? You send signals with your body. Lift your head, look directly at the person, and make some gesture toward that person. *As soon as you've raised your head, caught the person's eye and gestured, your interaction will have begun.*

We are now going to give you a series of tips in three specific areas that will enable you to become a good public speaker and have fun at the same time, regardless of how frightened or nervous you may think you are.

EYE CONTACT, POSTURE, AND MOVEMENT

1. **The first thing to remember in being a**

leader is to start the interaction. The person who begins the interaction is always the leader or status person, the dominant person in the seminar. The first thing you do to start an interaction is to stand up. This is the best rule for most of you. The general rule is to lift your heads, but it's a lot simpler to force yourself to stand. Many of you, if allowed to sit, will drop your heads. If you are standing, however, even if you drop your head a little, you are still in an erect posture. This doesn't mean you have to be a frozen ramrod. It means that you aren't hunched over, with head down, arms across your chest. This curled posture is the sign of submission, complete defeat. Keep your head up and reasonably straight. With your head up and in a standing position, you may have a slight slouch. This is a signal to everyone that you are casual and relaxed (even though that may not be the case).

2. **The second thing to do while standing up to your group is to look directly at them in turn.** As we said earlier, once you look at someone and catch his eye, you force him to respond to or interact with you. You have made the first move. Don't look at your notes, your instructor, the table, or your own shaking hands.

Before you begin talking, take a deep breath and casually look around at each person in your group. While you are talking, continue to glance at different people in your group as much as you can. Each time you look at someone you are forcing him to interact with you. In your notes you should have specific points you wish to bring to the attention of specific people in your audience. While you are addressing these people, look directly at them. Out of the corner of your eye you will notice that most of the people in the room are watching both of you, following what's going on. Don't underestimate the value of eye contact with everyone in your seminar. Shift your eyes around the room slowly but regularly so that you are forcing each person in the group to interact with you. Don't just look at one or two people. If you make this silly mistake you are signalling a cry for their support and approval (by their smiles and polite attention). You will automatically signal to everyone else in the room that you are no leader. They will undoubtedly turn off to you. After all, why should they pay attention to you? You obviously don't care about them, otherwise you would be looking at them too once in a while.

3. **The third thing you must do when you stand up to your group is move!** Remember if you will that a moving target is harder to hit. But moving is much more than just self-defense. There are four major aspects to moving:

(i) First, you want to control the people in your audience and in order to control them you have to capture their attention and keep it throughout your presentation. People automatically focus on something moving before they will look at something that is still. By moving you make your audience look at you.

(ii) Second — and just as important — is your leadership environment. *As a leader you have space. You must use this space by moving around in it, otherwise you are not behaving like a leader.* If you don't behave like a leader, if you try to take up a small space by not moving and by hunching over, you will loose your leadership role.

(iii) Third, if you move about and use your hands and arms to signal you are showing that you are involved in and excited about your topic. If you are involved and excited and are controlling others, they will become involved too. They will pay attention to what you are saying.

(iv) Finally, if you are moving, waving your hands and arms or your head, perhaps walking about in front of the room, the people in your seminar won't get bored. You must have some action to keep the seminar lively.

VOICE CONTROL

When standing up to your audience, your posture, eye contact, and movement created a situation in which you started the interaction and physically controlled most of what was going on in the room. But as you know, interaction also requires communication. As a leader you must take the initiative and perform the roles of providing information and opinion to your audience. After all, the main purpose is for you to teach them something. But as many of you know, it's not that easy. Many of you may have problems just speaking clearly. Here is a set of things for you to do when you talk that should enable you to continue to behave like a leader.

1. **If you are nervous, try not to be embarrassed by it.** Most people are nervous the first time they have to get up and speak. Many

teachers with twenty years of teaching or more behind them are nervous on the first day of classes. You are neither alone nor unique, just a normal student presenting a seminar. So joke about it if it will relax you. If your mouth is dry (and this is very common), bring some water to class. Every other public speaker has water nearby so why not you?

2. **Talk relatively softly and slowly.** Do not shout. This will strain your throat and make you very tired. If people can't hear, have them move closer. Do not talk above your normal conversational level. At the same time talking slowly forces you to pronounce words so you may speak more clearly.

3. **Try to work some feeling into your voice.** Many students presenting a seminar talk in a deadly monotone, never raising or lowering their voices or giving any emphasis or feeling to what they are saying. In your normal speaking voice, give some emphasis to your use of words. Have a few exclamation points and question marks in your voice. Get excited about what you are doing.

4. **Once you're talking to your audience and exchanging information, it is absolutely essential that you never read to them, unless it is a brief quote that is very important.** First of all, remember this is a seminar, not a recitation. *More importantly, every time a student starts to read a paper, the whole seminar falls apart.* Why? First of all, down goes the head. Then all movement stops. Eye contact stops as he reads from the paper. His voice flattens out to a monotone with little inflection and the reading speed picks up,

so that after a few minutes he is reading so fast no one can follow the presentation. At that point he is no longer a leader, just a source of background noise that everyone, including the instructor, turns off to. Never read a prepared speech or paper.

5. **Finally and most importantly, develop some feeling between you and your audience.** You are the leader and you have begun an interaction with these people to teach them something you find interesting. But in doing so, develop friendly relations with your group, some rapport. Don't be a cold puppet simply shouting words. Get them interested in your topic and involved with you. If you follow our tips on behavior and voice you will probably get the feeling you are talking the same way you would with a small group of close friends. Try to develop this feeling. When you get some warmth into your presentation, your audience will respond and your message and delivery will come across as warm and personal, not cold or phony. This will further involve your audience in your presentation.

ORGANIZATION AND TIMING

Now that we have you behaving and speaking like a leader, the only thing remaining in your seminar presentation is to make sure it goes smoothly for you and your audience. If you are following all of our suggestions, you should be putting on a pretty good presentation. You should have interesting material, with everyone involved in your topic. Things should be rolling right along.

Your presentation must move from one point to another smoothly and without long pauses. No fumbling, losing your place or your handouts, or forgetting which number on the board to point out please! This is one of the reasons we want you to practice your presentations. It is also why we told you to write down everything you want to do on your note cards. Remember, we even suggested writing down when to go to the board to point something out. If necessary, write down where that number is on the board so you can find it quickly and without embarrassment.

Timing and pace are everything. You must never lag, nor should you have to rush to get everything covered on time. *Therefore, in your first practice session notice exactly how many minutes each part of your presentation takes.* (For example, Introduction = 2 min. 20 sec.) The longest part of your presentation should be the two sections in which you present and discuss your facts. Here you will be using your visual aids. It is also the section that involves the most explanation. Your introduction should be the shortest section. Spend less than one fifth of your time on it. The sections on data and explanation should take up slightly more than half your time, perhaps a quarter for one and a third for the other. The remainder of your time should be spent on your conclusion.

In your practice runs if one of these sections is too long (i.e. if an introduction takes a quarter of your time), cut out some of the material. On your cards write down what time you should end each session, but make it approximate. You probably won't know ahead of time when you will start. However, if you do know you will start at about 10:15 a.m., you may note on your card that you should be through your introduction after three minutes, at about 10:18 a.m. When you reach a particular point in your presentation and realize you are ahead or behind your schedule, you may begin to adjust your pace so that you don't have to rush at the end. Remember, as with examinations, it's permissible to end ahead of time. You can always fill in spare time with questions. If you can't finish in time, however, you're in a real bind. If you hurry to get it done in time you will usually wind up leaving out important parts, with disastrous results for your mark.

With these points on timing you should be able to pace your presentation, get all your material in, and keep the presentation moving right along. But there are two more things you should do. *Always present your visual aids before you talk about what is in or on them.* If your aid contains a diagram that is part of your introduction, mention it, hand it out, or show it as soon as possible in the section so that your audience can look for it ahead of time. *Always warn your audience ahead of time that something important is coming up, such as a chart or table they will have to examine.* You can warn them by giving a slight preview at the beginning of each section. This gives them time to locate the material and look at it before you begin to discuss it. With this done, they won't get lost or confused. You are now all set to present your seminar. Good luck!

7 Starting the class discussion

Many students feel they have finished their seminar when they stop talking. Unfortunately this is not the case. A good seminar is one that starts other students talking. After all, the purpose has been to teach and the students should be ready to talk about what they have learned. If they aren't, your seminar has not been a success. **Always leave sufficient time for questions and discussion.**

We told you to mention several students (by name if necessary) in your presentation. If you have done this you should have several students who can't wait to start talking, either to correct you, defend themselves, or to put forth new ideas. Your seminar presentation should have primed the class for a discussion.

Your principal role now shifts from that of information and opinion giver to gatekeeper. You have a group of students who want to contribute. If each one has a chance to comment on your seminar, he or she will feel satisfied. If they don't get a chance to contribute, they will more than likely be upset and you can't have someone leaving the seminar angry. So you must be a strong gatekeeper, seeing to it that everyone who wants to talk gets a chance and making sure no one monopolizes the conversation. This includes you. Now is the time for you to ease yourself out of the spotlight. Let others take over the job of talking; you control the situation by calling on people, telling others to be quiet, etc.

There are two different types of comments students make after a seminar presentation: questions and discussion statements. One of your major problems will be to distinguish between them. A question usually means a student is looking for an explanation or clarification. He didn't understand some of your information or didn't see how you arrived at your conclusions. A statement on the other hand means a student is attempting to provide his own opinion or facts. Statements generally begin with the student stating what he thinks or knows. Then he implies that your data and conclusions aren't correct and forces you to defend yourself.

Always try to get the student questions out into the open and answered before you permit any discussion to begin. Your primary duty is to teach; therefore, you should be concerned with making sure that everyone in your seminar understood all your material. Permitting a discussion to start before everyone understands what you have said will also create bad feelings.

HOW TO ANSWER QUESTIONS

The first thing to remember about questions is that you will have to become a rather forceful gatekeeper. *Look for students who appear to be confused or hesitant,* those who might wish to ask a question but who are afraid to look stupid in front of the class. Once you have found them it is up to you to force the questions from them if necessary.

There are several things you may do to make sure you elicit all potential questions before you get into the discussion. You will recall when we mentioned the various small group roles, two of them were called information seeker and opinion seeker. These are people who are always asking questions. They may be doing it because they genuinely do not understand, or because they think someone in the class may not have understood but is too shy to ask, or just to get some attention. Regardless of why they ask questions you must keep an eye on the opinion or information seekers in your seminar. After you have finished speaking, ask the class if there are any questions. If there is no immediate response, turn to these seekers (if you have any in your class) and ask them directly if *they* have any questions. After you have dealt with their questions, look around the class. Is there anyone who looks confused or who might want to raise their hand but are hesitant? If you find anyone like this, ask him directly if he has any questions.

There are three more points about questions that must be mentioned. *First of all, if you are asked a question make sure you understand exactly what is being asked.* The question must be concerned with the material you have discussed in your presentation. If it asks for some form of clarification or explanation of the material you have presented, answer the question as simply as you can.

A rough question is a question that deals with the quality of your material. This type of question usually asks whether you had considered a particular approach, type of information, a particular person's work, etc. These are legitimate questions because they concern your references. A second form of rough question is the one that asks you whether or not you considered alternative explanations or conclusions that could have been derived from your information. This type of question concerns the quality of your logic, and both types are trouble for students. They must be answered, but at the same time they ask for more information and thought than you have probably covered in or considered for your presentation.

There are two ways to respond to rough questions. The first is to answer the question directly. You can do this if you have considered the material, information, or alternative conclusions and rejected them for valid reasons. Then simply tell your questioner you considered them and decided not to deal with them. Then list your reasons. If you had not considered them, and the whole issue is new to you, **admit that you hadn't considered the new point.** Then say you'd be interested in hearing about it from the questioner and **would they mind waiting a minute until all other questions have been asked and then giving the class more information about their point.** By doing this you shift the problem from yourself to the questioner and force him to provide information and opinion. Then you can ask *him* questions and avoid having to answer a question you are unprepared for.

Bad questions are always about something

not related to the material you have discussed. Try to avoid them during the question session. For example, you could get a question about divorced men or the effects of divorce on children after a presentation dealing with divorced women. Or after a presentation on sixteenth-century science and literature you get a question about modern scientific ethics, the Bomb, genetic research, or cruelty to lab animals. These questions have all been stimulated by your presentation but they have absolutely nothing to do with the material you presented or the conclusions you are trying to reach. **Do not answer them!** Don't even begin to deal with them during the question period. Bad questions are not questions at all, they are discussion statements. If someone asks you a bad question, state that it is an interesting point and ask the questioner to bring it up after everyone has had a chance to ask questions so the group may discuss it in more detail.

In conclusion, you must be an active and forceful gatekeeper during any question period. You must look for the students with questions and make sure that they understand the material and your conclusions. *The only questions you should consider are questions about your data and conclusions, questions that seek more information or clarification. If you get any questions that are rough or bad quickly write them down and use them as discussion statements later.*

STARTING A DISCUSSION

Your behavior in the discussion section of your

presentation should be slightly different from that of the questions part. Here you should try to be a quiet gatekeeper. Move into the background and let the other members of your seminar dominate the scene. **Your major activity should be to control who talks and for how long.**

You can easily get the discussion started. You have a number of people and issues waiting to discuss and be discussed. During your presentation you raised a number of points that were directed at specific individuals. These you have written down. Also, if you were fortunate you had some rough and bad questions during the question period. These were also written down. *The first thing you do is quickly review in your mind all these questions and points and pick the ones you think will be the most interesting and will get the most people talking.* **Then briefly read through all the points for the class and say something like, "Let's start with the point raised by Jim. Would you tell us a bit more about your point, Jim?"** Now withdraw and let Jim do the talking. **If things start to sag or it looks as if one topic is running down, jump in with the second most interesting issue you chose.** Say, "Well, it looks like we've covered that; what about Sally's point? Sally, would you mind telling us a bit more about that?"

Keep calling on people who have asked rough or bad questions or to whom you have directed parts of your presentation. In the worst of circumstances, where the people you directed parts of your presentation toward and the persons raising questions really don't have anything to say, it will take them at least two minutes each to say so. If you ask them particularly to review their points the responses of five persons will fill ten minutes. But if you have done your job properly the students in your seminar will have plenty to say.

Most of the people in your seminar should have read this book by now and realized it is in their own best interests to ask good questions or to take part in a minute or so of discussion. We have added a third section to this book, an important part on how to ask questions and make statements. Read it. Look at the next chapter for an outline to make sure you haven't missed anything.

8 An outline for preparing and presenting your seminar

Very few books contain a chapter in which all the major points are presented in outline form. We have chosen to do this for three reasons: first, now that we have completed our detailed description of how to prepare and present your seminar, an outline will help you get a good overall view of the total job. Too often, detailed manuals leave students so tied down in steps that they never really get an overview of what they're doing. We hope this chapter will help you see how each part fits into the whole, and keep each section in its proper perspective.

Second, an outline is a good way to review the material you have covered, refresh your memory, and make sure that you understand all the major points in preparing and presenting your summary.

But most important, this type of chapter gives you a complete checklist so you may plan everything for your seminar and make sure they get done on time and in the proper sequence. You won't find new information in this chapter but it could well be the most important chapter in the book.

(CHAPTER 1: SELECTING A GENERAL TOPIC)

A. *Select an interesting topic*
1. Use your own life, interests, or hunches as a starting point.

B. Selecting a topic from an assigned list
1. Read and define all topics in the list.
2. Are any topics related to any aspect of your past life or future plans?
3. Is there anything you recognize that you do or do not like?
4. As a last resort go to your instructor with your own topics (see C below).

C. Selecting your own topics
1. Get a course outline or the table of contents from your text.
2. Treat the outline or contents page exactly as you would an assigned list of topics. Repeat all the steps in B.

(CHAPTER 2: CREATING A SPECIFIC TOPIC FOR YOUR SEMINAR)

D. Narrowing and refining a topic
1. Create a working definition (or list of categories) for every major word in your topic.
2. Make a list of the definitions.
3. Pick a single definition from each list and combine the words into a sentence. (You may pick two or more words, but do so with caution.)
4. Always pick two specific topics.

(CHAPTER 3: GATHERING YOUR MATERIAL)

E. Using the library
1. Find out exactly what material is in the library (special collections, etc.).
2. Find out exactly where everything is located in the library. (Include special libraries.)
3. Learn the rules for using the library.

F. Gathering data
1. Define your topic in terms of the field's jargon.

(Look up the words in the topic in a special dictionary for the field.)

2. Get an overview of your topic. (Look up your topic in your field's handbooks and encyclopedias.)
3. Get the latest material. (Look in the indexes and abstracts for the latest journal articles on your topic.)
4. Use only books that are mentioned repeatedly in the journal articles.

G. Determine what material you will use

1. Read the entire journal article. (Do not take notes.)
2. Evaluate the article (quality of data, bias, etc.).
3. Locate specific bits of information you wish to use and take notes only on those specific items.

H. Simple notes

1. Use only index cards.
2. First card contains:
   a. Author, title, (journal, page for articles) and publication date.
   b. A five-line summary of book/article and whether it was useful or not.
3. Use a separate card for each specific bit of information or data table.
   a. At the top of each card write the author, publication date, and the page the bit of information was found on.

(CHAPTER 4: PREPARING YOUR SEMINAR)

I. Creating a theme or plan

1. Look at your data to see if the different articles and books have any similarities or specific differences.
2. Clarify the similarities or differences you find.
3. Decide if you wish to describe the similarities and differences or argue that one is superior to the other(s).

J. Organizing a logical presentation of your theme
1. All presentations have four parts:
   a. Introduction or problem (describes and introduces your topic).
      (i) Why you selected it.
      (ii) Why it is important.
      (iii) What your theme is (describe I above).
   b. Data presentation (your information is given to the class).
      (i) Decide the order you wish to present the information, which article will go first, second, etc.
      (ii) Decide on a specific order for talking about each article.
            1. You must use the same order for every article.
            2. You must talk about *only* the same material from each article.
      (iii) Plan to tell the audience your order (b(i) and (ii) above) before you present your information.
      (iv) Present your information only, do not make comments about it.
   c. Data explanation.
      (i) A general summary of what was found in the information.
            1. Do not make evaluative comments.
            2. You must use the same order as in your presentation.
   d. Conclusions.
      (i) Make evaluative statements about what your information proves or reveals and the value of what you have proved or shown.

K. Incoherent presentation, when you get off the topic
1. Check to make sure all points in J1 talk about the same thing and you haven't gotten off the topic.

L. Check understandability

1. Use simple, direct language.
   a. Use jargon as little as possible and explain in detail when you do so.

M. Visual aids
1. Simple outline of four sections (J1) must be presented to class.
2. Data and information should be illustrated with tables, graphs, etc.
3. Aids must be simple to make, use, and must contain simple messages.
4. Types of aids (decide on choice and check for problems in chapter four).
   a. Blackboard
   b. Posters
   c. Overhead projectors
   d. Handouts
   e. Slide and opaque projectors

N. Speaking notes
1. Get outline of presentation (J1).
2. Speaking notes are expanded outline.
   a. Get note cards (H3).
   b. Place individual note cards at appropriate points in outline.
   c. For areas with no note cards (problem, conclusion, J1, a and d), make note cards.
      (i) Go back to outline and make note cards.
3. Notes are just a deck of note cards arranged in proper order with one or two sheets of paper for the outline and perhaps other comments.
4. Underline major points in note cards so you can see them easily.
5. Never write out a speech word for word.

O. Written seminar report (if needed)
1. Take speaking notes (N3) and type or write them out filling in proper connecting sentences and phrases.

(CHAPTER 5: PREPARING TO SPEAK IN PUBLIC)

P. Planning to be a leader

1. Leaders start everything. Plan to start all action.
2. Think about members of your seminar.
   a. Various roles that people play in the seminar.
      (i) Link people to roles.
   b. Note problems in seminar that result from role conflict or lack of roles.
3. Plan to mention specific problems (quarrels, etc.) to the class so you may initiate action and control.
4. Plan to involve specific people having specific roles at particular points during your presentation, where you mention material that could be of interest to them.

Q. Make a leadership environment

1. Take the high ground. Get into the dominant position in the room.
2. Sit where you may look into each person's eyes.
3. Sit where you may easily reach all your aids without fumbling.

R. Final preparations

1. Make a leadership script.
   a. Make note cards of all leadership comments and actions (P3 and 4).
      (i) Insert cards in proper order in your deck of note cards.
   b. Make a diagram of the room, equipment, etc., so you know how and where to move.
2. Practice your presentation at least twice.

(CHAPTER 6: SPEAKING TO THE CLASS)

S. Acting like a leader

1. Stand up and look the class in the eye.
   a. Look at specific people and sweep the room.

2. Move around and use your hands if necessary to keep your audience's attention.

T. Talking
1. Bring something to drink to class.
2. Talk softly and slowly.
3. Get some expression into your voice.
   a. Emphasize major points (underlined, see N4 above).
4. Never read!
5. Talk to your seminar like you would a friend. Never talk *at* them.
6. Be informal and friendly; try to develop rapport.

U. Timing and organization
1. Time your practice (R2).
   a. Keep your eye on the time so you won't go over.
      (i) Perhaps insert flags into note cards that refer to time, so you are reminded to check it.
   b. If you are going overtime, switch to only underlined points (N4 above).
2. Always introduce your visual aids before you talk about them.
   a. Tell the seminar to look at the board, paper, etc.
3. Always warn the seminar ahead of time when you are going to talk about something important.
   a. Put a note on a note card and insert it in the right space.
4. Always begin a section with a brief description of what you will be talking about (a preview of coming attractions).
   a. Put a note card in the proper space.

(CHAPTER 7: STARTING THE CLASS DISCUS-
SION)

V. Discussions involve both questions and statements

1. Questions: they ask for an explanation or clarification.
   a. Look for students who appear confused or lost and ask if they have a question.
   b. Look for people with the role of questioner (P2a) and ask if they have a question.
   c. Make sure you understand the question; if not, ask that it be repeated.
   d. Rough questions are either those that criticize the quality of your material, or ask if you considered other themes or alternatives in your study.
      (i) You must answer them if you can.
      (ii) If you don't know the answer say so. Never try to fake it. Write them down and use them for discussion later.
   e. Bad questions are off the topic.
      (i) Don't answer. Write them down and use them for discussion later.
2. Statements are comments offered by members of your seminar.
   a. Review all rough and bad questions asked by members of seminar and all points you directed toward members during your presentation (P3 and 4) and pick the best.
      (i) On the paper, have the names of people and the points you plan to direct to them, during your presentation.
   b. Using the paper, go over all the rough questions and points for the class (a preview).
   c. Start with the most interesting and go down the list asking each person to comment.
      (i) As soon as one person has finished making a comment and the class has finished talking about it, move on to the next person.

PART III
SEMINAR
PARTICIPATION

9 How to be a good seminar member

A seminar is more than students getting up in front of a class and presenting material. Many students discover this when they receive an unpleasant surprise — their final grade. On page one we told you that the purpose of a seminar was to teach. The teacher and the lesson are only one half of teaching, even though they appear to dominate the situation. Just as important is having the students show that they have learned or at least are trying. Too many students never really find this out until they get a poor grade.

You participate in a seminar by learning. Now

that sounds simple enough. Every seminar has two aspects: teaching and learning. Both must occur if there is to be a good seminar. If students don't both learn and teach, they are not doing their job. *Finally, learning is demonstrated by what we call seminar participation.*

How does participation indicate learning? There are many ideas extant about what learning is but very little agreement about how it takes place or how to measure it. But most people would agree that the two necessities of learning are that the learner understands something and that he is able to use that thing. This is what you are tested on in exams and papers.

Understanding is the more subtle of these two aspects of learning. It is subtle because in universities and on the job understanding is up to you, not to the teacher. In elementary and secondary schools, teachers do everything they can to make sure you understand. Your university instructor or boss, however, gives you the material and it is up to you to make sure you understand. If you don't it is entirely your fault. You are responsible for your own understanding. How do you deal with this? Very simple: the same way your elementary and secondary school teachers suggested — ask questions when you don't understand something and keep asking them until you do.

Using the material is much easier. Once you understand the material being presented use it by trying to apply it to something that is slightly different from the examples used by the teacher. In other words, apply your knowledge. In arithmetic, after you learn the fractions ½ or ¼ you may show this by using these concepts to explain coins such as quarters or half-dollars. Use a new piece of information by making statements, raising points, or putting forth ideas (either pro or con) that show you have taken previous knowledge and put it to use to explain something new or to question what you have just learned.

By asking questions and making statements after the seminar presentation; you show you are learning.

HOW TO ASK QUESTIONS

When you ask a question you are adopting the role of either an information or opinion seeker. (We mentioned this in chapter five.) You don't necessarily have to be seeking the information or opinion yourself. You may quite easily be asking the questions for someone else, and thereby adopting the role of gatekeeper, coordinator, or orienter. Some of you may wonder about these roles. If you have a friend who is making the presentation and you notice he has missed a major point or has confused the audience, you may ask the question not because you have any lack of understanding but to help the presenter clarify his point. Or you may notice that someone looked very confused during the presentation, so try to help him out by asking a question to clarify his point.

Ask a question if you (or the class) do not understand a particular point. To get a clear understanding of what the speaker is talking about most students want either a further explanation of the point or some illustration or example showing how the point is used or what happens. For example, if I want to explain the word "science", I may give you either an explanation of the systematic examination of some phenomenon and try to explain that to you, or I may give you examples of what scientists have done and explain the word "science" by showing *what happens* in science. Most people when they run across something new like to have both an explanation and examples to make things crystal clear in their minds.

1. *The first thing you should do when you are asking a question is to decide whether you want an explanation or an example.*

2. The second thing to remember is to make certain that you talk directly to the person who made the presentation. Many students when they have a question ask the instructor. The instructor is *not* the seminar leader. The instructor should never answer a question unless the leader cannot.

3. The third thing you must do is to make absolutely certain that the seminar leader understands your question and knows what you're asking. As you know from your own seminar experience, when you are up there talking about your topic you don't always remember everything you said. So the person asking the question must be very careful to get all his facts straight. The best way to do this is to try and repeat what you remember the seminar leader had said. For example, you might say, "In the first part of your presentation you said that science was the systematic examination of a phenomenon." This gets the seminar leader on the same topic with

you. Now it might turn out that the seminar leader didn't say exactly that and you misinterpreted what was said. If so, by telling the leader what you thought was said, the confusion can be straightened out immediately. But if you did remember correctly and have a question, now that the leader knows exactly what part of the presentation you are talking about, the question may be answered.

4. The fourth part of asking questions is to be both specific and brief. Long, complicated questions never get properly answered. They serve only to turn off everyone in the seminar to you. Remember, you have decided whether to ask for more explanation, an example, or both; you have addressed the seminar leader directly; and you have made a specific reference to the presentation, so everyone knows exactly what you are talking about. Now, simply ask for further explanation or one or more examples.

HOW TO MAKE STATEMENTS

As with questions, we have a series of simple steps that will help you to make a contribution to a seminar.

1. The most important thing to remember when you want to make a point or express an idea in a discussion is that you must be relevant. *Your contribution must be concerned with the topic being discussed.* All too often we've seen students making fools of themselves, getting other people bored or angry by making silly, irrelevant statements. In many cases it is the seminar's

special-interest pleader who makes off-the-topic statements, trying to bend the seminar's topic into his own pet area. It is all too common to hear a special-interest pleader making a lengthy and irrelevant statement about the use of animals in experiments during a seminar on Shakespeare's treatment of scientists — particularly if someone happens to ask the question, "What is science?" Remember, if you want to make a contribution, make sure that what you say is relevant to the topic under discussion — otherwise, you may end up in trouble.

2. *Next, you must decide to whom you wish to make your comment.* If it is a comment to the entire seminar, try to sweep the room with your eyes, making contact with as many people as you can. This is the signal that the comment is addressed to all of them. If you decide that the comment is best directed to a specific individual — the seminar leader or a person who raised a question or made a comment — look at that person so that he knows it is up to him to respond.

3. The third rule for raising points in a discussion is that you must say *how* your point is relevant to the discussion. For example, if we are still on our Shakespeare and science seminar and you want to talk about present attitudes toward scientists, you should start by pointing out that, "Just as Shakespeare reflects the attitudes of his day, current movies and plays reflect our attitudes toward scientists and they are such and such, as you may easily see in the movie such and such." So, rule number three is build a bridge between your point or idea and some part of the presentation.

4. Get your idea out as quickly and simply

as possible. As a matter of fact, it is not necessarily a good idea to explain or justify your idea or point when you first raise it. What you should do is build your link to the presentation, then just make your point or state your idea. If people want to know more about it, or if they disagree with you, let them ask questions. When you answer these questions you may explain or prove your point.

5. After you have gotten your contribution out you have one final thing to do: place it in its proper perspective with regard to the topic. You have already built your bridge showing relevance and gotten your idea out. *Now you must specify whether your idea agrees or disagrees with the central ideas of the presentation.* After your idea is out simply say that it agrees with or disagrees with the specific point such and such raised by the presenter when he said such and such.

Now you have made a contribution to your seminar that everyone (including the presenter) may understand and handle. You have directed your comments to specific people forcing them to respond. You have shown exactly where your comment fits into the presentation by showing its relevance. You have presented the bare bones of your idea to get people interested. Finally, you have put your comment into proper perspective by showing exactly how it relates to the presentation.

MOT D'ESCALIER

This is one of our favorite French expressions. *Mot d'escalier*, "word of the stairs" — that perfect

comment or snappy reply you needed so desper-
ately in a class argument or discussion and the
one you remember only as you walk down the
stairs and out of the building! Unfortunately
many people think of questions and comments
only while walking out of the classroom. Don't let
this happen to you.

*During every presentation look for one major
point or statement you didn't clearly understand or that
you know something about and can disagree with or
support. Jot down this point and your comment
immediately.* (Never wait until the end of the
presentation.) Do this with every seminar, then
ask the question or make the comment after the
presentation is over. You will find that participating in seminars becomes easier, your learning
becomes a lot more fun, and your grades start to
improve!

Appendix A

These sourcebooks represent a very limited selection of the books available to help you in your search for seminar material. They are a place to start in your library. If your topic is not listed here, ask your librarian for Sheehy, E.P., GUIDE TO REFERENCE BOOKS, American Library Assn. (1976). This is the master guide to sourcebooks.

A BRIEF OUTLINE OF THE SUBJECTS COVERED IN THIS APPENDIX.

    3. Drama
  E. Fine arts
  F. Applied arts, theater arts, film, dance
  G. Music

III. Social Science
  A. General material and population statistics
  B. Anthropology, folklore and myth
  C. Economics
    1. Economics
    2. Business
  D. Education
  E. Geography
  F. Law
  G. Political science
    1. Political science
    2. International affairs
  H. Psychology
  I. Sociology

IV. Urban and environmental studies
  (pollution, architecture)

V. Natural sciences
  A. General material
  B. Biological sciences (botany, zoology, agriculture)
  C. Chemistry
  D. Earth sciences (geology, oceanography, hydrology, meteorology)
  E. Physics and mathematics (astronomy, space and engineering)
  F. Medical science

I. GENERAL MATERIAL
  a. Handbooks and encyclopedias
    Sheehy, E.P., GUIDE TO REFERENCE BOOKS, American Library Assn., 1976
  b. Indexes
    CANADIAN PERIODICAL INDEX

READER'S GUIDE TO PERIODICAL LITERATURE
SOCIAL SCIENCES AND HUMANITIES INDEX
after 1975 two indexes HUMANITIES INDEX
and SOCIAL SCIENCE INDEX

II. HUMANITIES

A. **Philosophy**

a. Guides to study and dictionaries

Borchardt, D.H., HOW TO FIND OUT IN PHI-
LOSOPHY AND PSYCHOLOGY, Pergamon,
1968

Brugger & Baker, PHILOSOPHICAL DICTIO-
NARY, Gonzaga, 1972

DeGeorge, R.T., A GUIDE TO PHILOSOPHICAL
BIBLIOGRAPHY AND RESEARCH,
Appleton-Century-Crofts, 1971

Wuellner, B., A DICTIONARY OF SCHOLASTIC
PHILOSOPHY (2nd ed.) Bruce, 1966

b. Handbooks and encyclopedias

Copelston, F. Ch., A HISTORY OF PHILOSO-
PHY, Newman, 1961

Edwards, P. (ed.), ENCYCLOPEDIA OF PHILOS-
OPHY, Macmillan, 1967

Grooten, J., NEW ENCYCLOPEDIA OF PHILOSO-
PHY, Philosophical, 1972

Hunnex, M., PHILOSOPHIES AND
PHILOSOPHERS (rev. ed.) Chandler, 1961

c. Indexes

THE PHILOSOPHER'S INDEX

B. **Religion**

a. Guides to study and dictionaries

Brandon (ed.), DICTIONARY OF COMPARA-
TIVE RELIGION, Scribner, 1970

Butterick (ed.), THE INTERPRETER'S DICTIO-
NARY OF THE BIBLE, Abington, 1962

Coss & Livingstone (eds.), THE OXFORD DIC-
TIONARY OF THE CHRISTIAN CHURCH, Oxford, 1974

Purvis, J.S., DICTIONARY OF ECCLESIASTICAL

TERMS, Nelson, 1962
b. Handbooks and encyclopedias
  Gibb et al. (eds.), ENCYCLOPEDIA OF ISLAM, Brill, 1975
  Harvey, V.A., A HANDBOOK OF THEOLOGICAL TERMS, Macmillan, 1964
  Loetscher (ed.), TWENTIETH CENTURY ENCYCLOPEDIA OF RELIGIOUS KNOWLEDGE, Baker, 1955
  Malalasekera (ed.), ENCYCLOPEDIA OF BUDDHISM, Sri Lanka Govt., 1972
  Mead, F.S., HANDBOOK OF DENOMINATIONS IN THE UNITED STATES, Abington, 1970
  Negev, Abraham (ed.), ARCHAEOLOGICAL ENCYCLOPEDIA OF THE HOLY LAND, Putnam's, 1972
  Orr, James (ed.), INTERNATIONAL STANDARD BIBLE ENCYCLOPEDIA, Eerdmans, 1960
  Walker, B., HINDU WORLD: AN ENCYCLOPEDIA SURVEY OF HINDUISM, Praeger, 1968
  ENCYCLOPAEDIA JUDAICA, Macmillan, 1972
c. Indexes
  INDEX TO RELIGIOUS PERIODICAL LITERATURE
  RELIGIOUS AND THEOLOGICAL ABSTRACTS
C. History and area studies
1. General history
  a. Guides to study and dictionaries
    Hepworth, P., HOW TO FIND OUT IN HISTORY: A GUIDE TO SOURCES OF INFORMATION FOR ALL, Pergamon, 1966
    Rodriguez, M. and Peloso, V.C., A GUIDE FOR THE STUDY OF CULTURE IN CENTRAL AMERICA, Pan American Union, 1968
    Shafer, R.J., A GUIDE TO HISTORICAL METHOD, Dorsey, 1974
  b. Handbooks and encyclopedias
    Morris, R.B. and Irwin, G.W., HARPER EN-

CYCLOPEDIA OF THE MODERN WORLD, Harper, 1970

Palmer, R.D., ATLAS OF WORLD HISTORY, Rand McNally, 1957

c. Indexes

ANNUAL BULLETIN OF HISTORICAL LITERATURE

HISTORICAL ABSTRACTS

INTERNATIONAL BIBLIOGRAPHY OF HISTORICAL SCIENCES

2. Archeology, classics

a. Guides to study and dictionaries

Hammond and Scullard (ed.), THE OXFORD CLASSICAL DICTIONARY, Clarendon Press, 1970

b. Handbooks and encyclopedias

Cottrell, L. (ed.), CONCISE ENCYCLOPEDIA OF ARCHAEOLOGY, Hawthorn, 1970

Tripp, (ed.), CROWELL'S HANDBOOK OF CLASSICAL MYTHOLOGY, Crowell, 1970

THE CAMBRIDGE ANCIENT HISTORY, Cambridge University Press

Heyden (ed.), ATLAS OF THE CLASSICAL WORLD, Nelson, 1963

Thomson, J.O., EVERYMAN'S CLASSICAL ATLAS, (3rd ed.), Dutton, 1961

c. Indexes

ARCHAEOLOGICAL REPORTS ANNUAL (handbook)

3. North America

a. Guides to study and dictionaries

Adams, James T. (ed.), DICTIONARY OF AMERICAN HISTORY, Scribner's, 1961

Boatner, Mark Mayo, THE CIVIL WAR DICTIONARY, 1969

Campbell, H.C., HOW TO FIND OUT ABOUT CANADA, 1967

b. *Handbooks and encyclopedias*

Bray, W. and Trump, D., THE AMERICAN HERITAGE GUIDE TO ARCHAEOLOGY, American Heritage, 1970

Carruth, G., THE ENCYCLOPEDIA OF AMERICAN FACTS AND DATES, Crowell, 1972

Robbins, J.E. (ed.), ENCYCLOPEDIA CANADIANA, Grolier, 1970

WEBSTER'S GUIDE TO AMERICAN HISTORY: A CHRONOLOGICAL, GEOGRAPHICAL AND BIOGRAPHICAL SURVEY & COMPENDIUM, G & C Merriam, 1971

4. England

a. *Guides to study and dictionaries*

Steinberg, S.H., A NEW DICTIONARY OF BRITISH HISTORY, E. Arnold, 1963

b. *Handbooks and encyclopedias*

Brooke, C.N.L. and Smith, D.M. (eds.), A HISTORY OF ENGLAND, Nelson, 1961

Cheney, C.R., HANDBOOK OF DATES FOR STUDENTS OF ENGLISH HISTORY, Royal Historical Society, 1945

Clark, G.N. (ed.), THE OXFORD HISTORY OF ENGLAND (15 vol.), Clarendon

Medlicott, W.N. (ed.), A HISTORY OF ENGLAND (10 vol.), Longmans

Martin, G., BRITISH HISTORY ATLAS, Macmillan, 1969

5. Europe

b. *Handbooks and encyclopedias*

Adams, et al., AN ATLAS OF RUSSIAN AND EAST EUROPEAN HISTORY, Praeger, 1967

Bezer, C.A. (ed.), RUSSIAN AND SOVIET STUDIES: A HANDBOOK, Columbia Univ. Russian Instit. Amer. Ass. Adv. Slavic Studies, 1973

Bithell, J., GERMANY: A COMPANION TO GERMAN STUDIES, (5th ed.), Methuen, 1955

Calmann, John, WESTERN EUROPE: A HAND-
BOOK, Praeger, 1967

Chew, A.F., AN ATLAS OF RUSSIAN HISTORY
(rev. ed.), Yale Univ. Pr., 1970

Clapham & Powers (eds.), CAMBRIDGE ECO-
NOMIC HISTORY OF EUROPE, Cambridge
Univ. Pr.

Jelavich, C. (ed.), EAST CENTRAL AND SOUTH-
EASTERN EUROPE: A SURVEY, University of
Chicago, 1969

Roucek, J.S. (ed.), SLAVONIC ENCYCLOPEDIA,
Philosophical Lib., 1969

Schopflin, G. (ed.), SOVIET UNION AND EAST-
ERN EUROPE: A HANDBOOK, 1970

MCGRAW-HILL ENCYCLOPEDIA OF RUSSIA AND
THE SOVIET UNION, McGraw-Hill, 1961

c. Indexes

REVIEWS IN EUROPEAN HISTORY, Redgrave
Info. Resources Co., Westport, Conn.

6. Africa

b. Handbooks and encyclopedias

Face, J.D., AN ATLAS OF AFRICAN HISTORY, E.
Arnold, 1958

Legum, C. (ed.), AFRICA: A HANDBOOK TO
THE CONTINENT (rev. ed.) Praeger, 1966

Lystad, R.A. (ed.), THE AFRICAN WORLD, A
SURVEY OF SOCIAL RESEARCH, Praeger,
1965

c. Indexes

U.S. Library of Congress, RESEARCH AND
INFORMATION ON AFRICA: CONTINUING
SOURCES, Washington, D.C.

7. Asia

a. Handbooks and encyclopedias

Bhattacharya, S., A DICTIONARY OF INDIAN
HISTORY, Braziller, 1967

Hall, J.W., JAPANESE HISTORY: A GUIDE TO
JAPANESE REFERENCE MATERIALS, Univer-

sity of Michigan, 1954

Johnson, D.C., A GUIDE TO REFERENCE MATERIALS ON SOUTHEAST ASIA, Yale University Press, 1970

Nunn, G.R., ASIA: A SELECTED AND ANNOTATED GUIDE TO REFERENCE WORKS, Harvard University Press, 1971

Papinot, E., HISTORICAL AND GEOGRAPHICAL DICTIONARY OF JAPAN, Ungar, 1964

Patterson, M.L.P. and Inden, R.B., SOUTHEAST ASIA: AN INTRODUCTORY BIBLIOGRAPHY, University of Chicago Press, 1962

b. Handbooks and encyclopedias

CAMBRIDGE HISTORY OF INDIA (6 vol.), Cambridge Univ. Press

Wu-Yuan-Li, CHINA: A HANDBOOK, Praeger, 1973

Sauvaget, J., INTRODUCTION TO THE HISTORY OF THE MUSLIM EAST: A BIBLIOGRAPHICAL GUIDE, 1965

Ronart, S. and Ronart, N., CONCISE ENCYCLOPEDIA OF ARABIC CIVILIZATION: ARAB EAST AND ARAB WEST (2 vol.), 1966

Osborne, C., AUSTRALIA, NEW ZEALAND AND THE SOUTH PACIFIC: A HANDBOOK, Praeger, 1970

D. **Literature**

1. General works and prose

a. Guides to study and dictionaries

Barnet and Burto, A DICTIONARY OF LITERARY, DRAMATIC AND CINEMATIC TERMS, Little, Brown, 1971

Bateson, F.W. et al., A GUIDE TO ENGLISH AND AMERICAN LITERATURE (3rd ed.), Longman, 1976

Beckson, K.E., LITERARY TERMS: A DICTIONARY (rev. ed.), Farrar, Straus and Giroux, 1975

Bell and Gallup, A REFERENCE GUIDE TO ENGLISH, AMERICAN AND CANADIAN LITERATURE, Univ. of British Columbia, 1971

Bleznick, D.W., A SOURCEBOOK FOR HISPANIC LITERATURE AND LANGUAGE: GUIDE TO SPANISH AND SPANISH-AMERICAN BIBLIOGRAPHY, LITERATURE, LINGUISTICS, JOURNALS AND OTHER MATERIALS, Temple, 1974

British Columbia University Library, A CHECKLIST OF PRINTED MATERIALS RELATING TO FRENCH-CANADIAN LITERATURE, 1763-1968, University of British Columbia, 1973

Eagle, D., CONCISE OXFORD DICTIONARY OF ENGLISH LITERATURE, Clarendon, 1970

Foster, D.W., THE 20TH CENTURY SPANISH-AMERICAN NOVEL: A BIBLIOGRAPHIC GUIDE, Scarecrow, 1975

Holman, C.H., HANDBOOK TO LITERATURE, Dorsey Press, 1972

Jones, H.M., GUIDE TO AMERICAN LITERATURE AND ITS BACKGROUNDS SINCE 1890 (4th ed.), Duke, 1976

Leary, L.G. et. al., AMERICAN LITERATURE: A STUDY AND RESEARCH GUIDE, St. Martins, 1976

Moyles, R.G., ENGLISH-CANADIAN LITERATURE: A STUDENT GUIDE AND ANNOTATED BIBLIOGRAPHY, Athabascan, 1972

Shaw, Harry, DICTIONARY OF LITERARY TERMS, McGraw-Hill, 1972

b. *Handbooks and encyclopedias*

Barnhart, C.L. (ed.), NEW CENTURY HANDBOOK OF ENGLISH LITERATURE, Appleton, 1967

Benet, W.R., THE READER'S ENCYCLOPEDIA, Crowell, 1965

Buchanan-Brown, J., CASSELL'S ENCYC-
LOPAEDIA OF WORLD LITERATURE, Cassell,
1973

Holman, C.H., A HANDBOOK TO LITERATURE,
Odyssey, 1972

Story, N., THE OXFORD COMPANION TO
CANADIAN HISTORY AND LITERATURE
1967, Supplement 1973, Oxford Univ.
Press

Vinson, J. (ed.), CONTEMPORARY NOVELISTS,
St. Martin's, 1972

THE PENGUIN COMPANION TO WORLD LITER-
ATURE, McGraw-Hill, 1971

c. *Indexes*

Cook, D. and Monro, I., SHORT STORY INDEX,
Wilson, 1953

Day, D.B., INDEX TO THE SCIENCE-FICTION
MAGAZINES, 1926-1950, Perri, 1952

Siemon, F., SCIENCE FICTION STORY INDEX,
1950-1968, Amer. Lib. Assoc., 1971

ABSTRACTS OF ENGLISH STUDIES

A.L.A. INDEX TO GENERAL LITERATURE

ANNUAL BIBLIOGRAPHY OF ENGLISH LAN-
GUAGE AND LITERATURE

M.L.A. INTERNATIONAL BIBLIOGRAPHY OF
BOOKS, ARTICLES, (also known as P.M.L.A.
BIBLIOGRAPHY)

2. Poetry

a. *Guides to study and dictionaries*

Deutsch, POETRY HANDBOOK: A DICTIONARY
OF TERMS, Funk & Wagnall, 1974

b. *Handbooks and encyclopedias*

Malkoff, K., CROWELL'S HANDBOOK OF CON-
TEMPORARY AMERICAN POETRY, Crowell,
1973

Murphy, R. (ed.), CONTEMPORARY POETS OF
THE ENGLISH LANGUAGE, St. James, 1970

Preminger, A. (ed.), ENCYCLOPEDIA OF POETRY AND POETICS, Princeton, 1965

Spender, S. and Hall, D., THE CONCISE ENCYCLOPEDIA OF ENGLISH AND AMERICAN POETS AND POETRY, Hawthorn, 1963

c. Indexes

INDEX OF AMERICAN PERIODICAL VERSE, Scarecrow, 1973

Sell, Violet et al., AMERICAN LIBRARY ASSOCIATION, SUBJECT INDEX TO POETRY FOR CHILDREN AND YOUNG PEOPLE, A.L.A., 1957

3. Drama

b. Handbooks and encyclopedias

Adelman, I. and Dworkin, R., MODERN DRAMA: A CHECKLIST OF CRITICAL LITERATURE ON 20TH CENTURY PLAYS, Scarecrow, 1967

Anderson, M. et al., CROWELL'S HANDBOOK OF CONTEMPORARY DRAMA, Crowell, 1971

Grismer, R.L., BIBLIOGRAPHY OF THE DRAMA OF SPAIN AND SPANISH AMERICA, Burgess-Beckwith, 1967

Matlaw, M., MODERN WORLD DRAMA: AN ENCYCLOPEDIA, Dutton, 1972

MCGRAW-HILL ENCYCLOPEDIA OF WORLD DRAMA, McGraw-Hill, 1972

c. Indexes

Breed, P. and Sniderman, F., DRAMATIC CRITICISM INDEX, Gale, 1972

Faxon, Bates and Sutherland, CUMULATED DRAMATIC INDEX, G.K. Hall, 1965

Keller, D., INDEX TO PLAYS IN PERIODICALS, Scarecrow, 1971

Ottemiller, J.H., OTTEMILLER'S INDEX TO PLAYS IN COLLECTIONS, Scarecrow, 1971

E. **Fine arts**

a. Guides to study and dictionaries

Chamberlin, M.W., GUIDE TO ART REFERENCE BOOKS, Amer. Lib. Assoc., 1959

Mayer, R., A DICTIONARY OF ART TERMS AND TECHNIQUES, Crowell, 1969

Murray and Murray, A DICTIONARY OF ART AND ARTISTS, Praeger, 1965

Myers, B.S. (ed.), MCGRAW-HILL DICTIONARY OF ART, McGraw-Hill, 1969

Taubes, F., THE PAINTER'S DICTIONARY OF MATERIALS AND METHODS, Watson-Guptill, 1971

b. *Handbooks and encyclopedias*

Mayer, R., THE ARTIST'S HANDBOOK OF MATERIALS AND TECHNIQUES, Viking Press, 1970

Myers, B.S. (ed.), ENCYCLOPEDIA OF PAINTING, Crown, 1955

ENCYCLOPEDIA OF WORLD ART, McGraw-Hill, 1968

c. *Indexes*

ART INDEX

Clapp, J., SCULPTURE INDEX, Scarecrow, 1971

F. **Applied arts, theater arts, film, dance**

a. *Guides to study and dictionaries*

Balanchine, G., BALANCHINE'S NEW COMPLETE STORIES OF THE GREAT BALLETS, Doubleday, 1968

Boger and Boger, THE DICTIONARY OF ANTIQUES AND THE DECORATIVE ARTS, Scribner's, 1967

Brockett, Becker and Bryant, A BIBLIOGRAPHICAL GUIDE TO RESEARCH IN SPEECH AND DRAMATIC ART, Scott, Foresman, 1963

Cunnington, Cunnington and Beard, A DICTIONARY OF ENGLISH COSTUME (900-1900), Dufour, 1960

Kersley, L. and Sinclair, J., A DICTIONARY OF BALLET TERMS, Pitman, 1960

Kienzle, S., MODERN WORLD THEATER: A GUIDE TO PRODUCTIONS IN EUROPE AND THE UNITED STATES SINCE 1945, UNGAR, 1970

Manchel, F., FILM STUDY: A RESOURCE GUIDE, Fairleigh Dickinson, 1973

Spencer, D.A., THE FOCAL DICTIONARY OF PHOTOGRAPHIC TECHNOLOGIES, Prentice-Hall, 1973

Taylor, J.R., THE PENGUIN DICTIONARY OF THE THEATRE, Penguin, 1966

b. Handbooks and encyclopedias

Aronson, J., THE ENCYCLOPEDIA OF FURNITURE, Crown, 1965

Cawkwell, T. and Smith, J., THE WORLD ENCYCLOPEDIA OF THE FILM WORLD, Studio Vista, 1972

Chujoy, A. and Manchester, P., THE DANCE ENCYCLOPEDIA, Simon & Schuster, 1967

Gassner, J. and Quinn, E., THE READER'S ENCYCLOPEDIA OF WORLD DRAMA, Crowell, 1969

Heffner, H.C., et. al., MODERN THEATRE PRACTICE, (5th ed.) Appleton, 1972

Ramsey, G.G., (CONNOISSEUR) THE COMPLETE ENCYCLOPEDIA OF ANTIQUES, Hawthorn, 1962

Sobel, B., THE NEW THEATRE HANDBOOK AND DIGEST OF PLAYS, 1959

FOCAL ENCYCLOPEDIA OF PHOTOGRAPHY, Focal Pr., 1965

INTERNATIONAL ENCYCLOPEDIA OF THE FILM, Crown, 1972

c. Indexes

Guernsey, O.L., DIRECTORY OF THE AMERICAN THEATER, 1894-1971, Dodd, Mead, 1971

Monro, I. and Cook, D., COSTUME INDEX: A

SUBJECT INDEX TO PLATES AND TO ILLUS-
TRATED TEXTS, Wilson, 1937

Sharp, H.S. and Sharp, M.Z., INDEX TO
CHARACTERS IN THE PERFORMING ARTS,
Scarecrow, 1972

FILM LITERATURE INDEX, Filmdex Inc.

GUIDE TO DANCE PERIODICALS, Univ. of
Florida Pr., 1963

GUIDE TO THE PERFORMING ARTS, Scarecrow

G. Music

a. Guides to study and dictionaries

Ammer, C., HARPER'S DICTIONARY OF MUSIC,
Harper & Row, 1972

Apel, W., HARVARD DICTIONARY OF MUSIC,
(2nd ed.), Harvard, 1969

Davies, J.H., MUSICALIA: SOURCES OF INFOR-
MATION IN MUSIC, Oxford, 1969

Watanabe, R.R., INTRODUCTION TO MUSIC
RESEARCH, Prentice-Hall, 1967

b. Handbooks and encylopedias

Berkowitz, F.P., POPULAR TITLES AND SUBTI-
TLES OF MUSICAL COMPOSITIONS, Scarecrow, 1962

Thompson, O. and Sabin, R. (eds.), THE
INTERNATIONAL ENCYCLOPEDIA OF MUSIC
AND MUSICIANS, (9th ed.), Dodd, 1964

c. Indexes

Belknap, S.Y., GUIDE TO THE MUSICAL ARTS:
AN ANALYTICAL INDEX OF ARTICLES AND
ILLUSTRATIONS, Scarecrow, 1957

III. SOCIAL SCIENCE

A. General material and population statistics

*Note: For social science areas students should always
check the general material as well as the material
listed under specific areas.*

a. Guides to study and dictionaries

Gould, J. (ed.), A DICTIONARY OF THE SOCIAL
SCIENCES, Free Press, 1964

Hoselitz, B.F., A READER'S GUIDE TO THE SOCIAL SCIENCES, Free Press, 1970

Lewis, P.R., THE LITERATURE OF THE SOCIAL SCIENCES, Lib. Assoc., 1960

Stevens, R.E., REFERENCE BOOKS IN THE SOCIAL SCIENCES AND HUMANITIES, Illini Union Bookstore, 1968

  b. Handbooks and encyclopedias

Sills, D.L. (ed.), INTERNATIONAL ENCYCLOPEDIA OF THE SOCIAL SCIENCES, Macmillan, 1968, Old Version: ENCYCLOPEDIA OF THE SOCIAL SCIENCES

  c. Indexes

THE ABS GUIDE TO RECENT PUBLICATIONS IN THE SOCIAL AND BEHAVIOURAL SCIENCES, Amer. Behavioural Scientist

P.A.I.S. (Public Affairs Information Service Bulletin), (*Major Current Social Science Index for World*)

SOCIAL SCIENCE ABSTRACTS

SOCIAL SCIENCE CITATION INDEX

SOCIAL SCIENCE INDEX

1. Population Statistics

  a. Guides to study and dictionaries

Andriot, J.L., GUIDE TO U.S. GOVERNMENT STATISTICS (4th ed.), Documents Index, 1973

Freund, J.E. and Williams, F.J., DICTIONARY/OUTLINE OF BASIC STATISTICS, McGraw-Hill, 1966

Harvey, J.M., SOURCES OF STATISTICS, Linnet Books & Clive Bingly, 1971

INTER-AMERICAN STATISTICAL INSTITUTE STATISTICAL VOCABULARY, (2nd ed.), Pan Amer. Union

INTERNATIONAL UNION FOR THE SCIENTIFIC STUDY OF POPULATION MULTILINGUAL DEMOGRAPHIC DICTIONARY, United Nations, Dept. of Economic and Social Affairs, 1958

Wasserman, P. and Paskar, J. (eds.), STATISTICS SOURCES (4th ed.), Gale, 1974

b. Handbooks and encyclopedias

CANADA YEARBOOK

DEMOGRAPHIC YEARBOOK, Statistical Office, United Nations

SOUTH AMERICAN HANDBOOK, A yearbook and guide to the countries and resources of South and Central America, Mexico and West Indies, Trade and Travel Pb.

STATISTICAL YEARBOOK, Unesco

c. Indexes

AMERICAN STATISTICS INDEX, Congressional Info. Serv., 1973

POPULATION INDEX, Office of Population Research, Princeton

B. **Anthropology**

a. Guides to study and dictionaries

Frantz, C., THE STUDENT ANTHROPOLOGIST'S HANDBOOK: A GUIDE TO RESEARCH, Schenkman, 1972

Thompson, S., THE FOLKTALE: A GUIDE, Dryden Pr., 1946

Winick, C., DICTIONARY OF ANTHROPOLOGY, Philosophical, 1956

INTERNATIONAL DICTIONARY OF REGIONAL EUROPEAN ETHNOLOGY AND FOLKLORE, Rosenkilde & Bagger, 1960

b. Handbooks and encyclopedias

Coon, C.S., THE ORIGIN OF RACES, Knopf, 1962

Honigmann, J.J., HANDBOOK OF SOCIAL AND CULTURAL ANTHROPOLOGY, Rand McNally, 1973

Hunter, D.C. and Whitten, P., ENCYCLOPEDIA OF ANTHROPOLOGY, Harper and

Row, 1976

Radford and Radford, ENCYCLOPEDIA OF
SUPERSTITION, Hutchinson, 1961

Robbins, R.H., THE ENCYCLOPEDIA OF
WITCHCRAFT AND DEMONOLOGY, Crown,
1959

Siegel, B.J. (ed.), BIENNIAL REVIEW OF AN-
THROPOLOGY 1959-71, ANNUAL REVIEW OF
ANTHROPOLOGY, 1972 to present

c. Indexes

Cleveland Public Library (John G. White
Dept.), CATALOG OF FOLKLORE AND FOLK
SONGS (110,000 listings), G.K. Hall, 1964

Royal Anthropological Institute of Great
Britain and Ireland Library, INDEX TO
CURRENT PERIODICALS, 1962

ABSTRACTS OF FOLKLORE STUDIES

INTERNATIONAL BIBLIOGRAPHY OF SOCIAL
AND CULTURAL ANTHROPOLOGY

C. **Economics**

1. Economics

a. Guides to study and dictionaries

Fletcher, J., THE USE OF ECONOMICS LITERA-
TURE, Archon Books, 1971

Greenwald, D. (ed.), MCGRAW-HILL DICTIO-
NARY OF MODERN ECONOMICS, (2nd ed.),
McGraw-Hill, 1973

Sloan, H.S. and Zurcher, A., DICTIONARY OF
ECONOMICS, (5th ed.), Barnes and Noble

b. Handbooks and encylopedias

U.N. Department of Economic and Social
Affairs, WORLD ECONOMIC REVIEW

c. Indexes

INDEX OF ECONOMIC ARTICLES, 1971

ECONOMIC ABSTRACTS

2. Business: General

a. Guides to study and dictionaries

Alexander Hamilton Institute, A.H.I. 2001

BUSINESS TERMS AND WHAT THEY MEAN, 1962

Coman, E.T., SOURCES OF BUSINESS INFORMATION, UCLA, 1964

CCH, LABOUR TERMS, CCH, 1955

Gazurian, J.A., THE ADVERTISING AND GRAPHIC ARTS GLOSSARY, Los Angeles Trade-Tech. College, 1966

Harvard G.S.B.A., BUSINESS REFERENCE SOURCES, Harvard (Baker Lib.), 1971

Kohler, E.L., A DICTIONARY FOR ACCOUNTANTS, (4th ed.), Prentice Hall, 1970

Lindemann, A.J., et al., DICTIONARY OF MANAGEMENT TERMS, W.C. Brown, 1966

ENCYCLOPEDIC DICTIONARY OF BUSINESS FINANCE, Prentice-Hall, 1961

b. Handbooks and encyclopedias

Badger, R.E., THE COMPLETE GUIDE TO INVESTMENT ANALYSIS, McGraw-Hill, 1967

Barton, R., HANDBOOK OF ADVERTISING, McGraw-Hill, 1970

Famularo, J.J. (ed.), HANDBOOK OF MODERN PERSONNEL ADMINISTRATION, McGraw-Hill, 1972

Farrell, M.L. (ed.), THE DOW JONES INVESTOR'S HANDBOOK (Annual), Dow Jones Book

Graham, I., ENCYCLOPEDIA OF ADVERTISING, (2nd ed.), Fairchild

Heyel, C., THE ENCYCLOPEDIA OF MANAGEMENT, (2nd ed.), Van Nostrand, 1973

Kraus, A.L., THE N.Y. TIMES GUIDE TO BUSINESS AND FINANCE: THE AMERICAN ECONOMY AND HOW IT WORKS, Harper & Row, 1972

Lesly, P., LESLY'S PUBLIC RELATIONS HANDBOOK, Prentice-Hall, 1971

Maynard, H.B. (ed.), HANDBOOK OF BUSINESS

ADMINISTRATION, McGraw-Hill, 1967

Munn, G.G., ENCYCLOPEDIA OF BANKING AND FINANCE, (6th ed.), Banker's Pub. Co. 1962

Richard, J.M., A GUIDE TO ADVERTISING INFORMATION, MacDougal, 1969

Wasserman, P. (ed.), ENCYCLOPEDIA OF BUSINESS INFORMATION SOURCES, Gale, 1970

Yoder, D., et al., HANDBOOK OF PERSONAL MANAGEMENT AND LABOUR RELATIONS, McGraw-Hill, 1958

ACCOUNTANTS' HANDBOOK, Ronald, 1970

FINANCIAL POST SURVEYS OF CANADIAN BUSINESS

HANDBOOK OF MODERN ACCOUNTING, McGraw-Hill, 1970

c. Indexes

American Institute of Certified Public Accountants, ACCOUNTANTS' INDEX

National Industrial Conference Board, CUMULATIVE INDEX

BUSINESS PERIODICALS INDEX

EMPLOYMENT RELATIONS ABSTRACTS, Information Service

INDEX TO LABOR ARTICLES, Rand School of Social Science

INTERNATIONAL REVIEW OF ADMINISTRATIVE SCIENCES

D. Education

a. Guides to study and dictionaries

Good, C.V., DICTIONARY OF EDUCATION, McGraw-Hill, 1973

b. Handbooks and encyclopedias

Blishen, E., (ed.), ENCYCLOPEDIA OF EDUCATION, Philosophical, 1970

Deighton, L.C. (ed.), ENCYCLOPEDIA OF EDUCATION, Macmillan, 1971

Ebel, R.L. (ed.), ENCYCLOPEDIA OF EDUCA-

TIONAL RESEARCH, Macmillan, 1969

Hillway, T., HANDBOOK OF EDUCATIONAL RESEARCH: A GUIDE TO METHODS AND MATERIALS, Houghton, 1969

Smith, Aker, and Kidd, HANDBOOK OF ADULT EDUCATION, Macmillan, 1970

c. Indexes

BRITISH EDUCATION INDEX

CANADIAN EDUCATION INDEX

CHILD DEVELOPMENT ABSTRACTS AND BIBLIOGRAPHY

CURRENT INDEX TO JOURNALS IN EDUCATION, CCM Information Sciences

EDUCATION ABSTRACTS, UNESCO Educ. Clearing House

EDUCATION INDEX, Wilson

RESEARCH IN EDUCATION (Educational Research Information Center *ERIC*), U.S. Dept., H.E.W.

E. **Geography**

a. Guides to study and dictionaries

Alexander, G.L., GUIDE TO ATLASES: WORLD, REGIONAL, NATIONAL, THEMATIC, AN INTERNATIONAL LISTING OF ATLASES PUBLISHED SINCE 1950

Durrenberger, R.W., GEOGRAPHICAL RESEARCH AND WRITING, Crowell, 1971

Martinson, T.L., INTRODUCTION TO LIBRARY RESEARCH IN GEOGRAPHY: AN INSTRUCTION MANUAL AND SHORT BIBLIOGRAPHY

Monkhouse, F.J., A DICTIONARY OF GEOGRAPHY, 1970

Schmieder, A.A. et al., A DICTIONARY OF BASIC GEOGRAPHY, Allyn & Bacon, 1970

b. Handbooks and encyclopedias

Lock, C.B.M., GEOGRAPHY AND CARTOGRAPHY: A REFERENCE HANDBOOK, Ringley, 1976

c. *Indexes*

American Geographical Society, INDEX TO MAPS IN BOOKS AND PERIODICALS

ARCTIC BIBLIOGRAPHY, Arctic Institute of North America

CURRENT GEOGRAPHICAL PUBLICATIONS, Annual

GEO ABSTRACTS

F. **Law**

a. *Guide to study and dictionaries*

Black, H.C., BLACK'S LAW DICTIONARY, West, 1957

b. *Handbooks and encyclopedias*

King, Samuel G., THE COMPLETE GUIDE TO EVERYDAY LAW, (2nd ed.), Follett, 1970

Landau, N.J. and Rheingold, P.D.., THE ENVIRONMENTAL LAW HANDBOOK, Ballantine, 1971

National Institute for Education in Law and Poverty, HANDBOOK ON CONSUMER LAW, Northwestern, 1968

Prentice-Hall (ed.), ENCYCLOPEDIC DICTIONARY OF BUSINESS LAW, Prentice-Hall, 1961

AMERICAN JURISPRUDENCE (ANNUAL), Lawyers Co-operative

c. *Indexes*

INDEX TO CANADIAN LEGAL PERIODICAL LITERATURE

INDEX TO LEGAL PERIODICALS

INDEX TO PERIODICAL ARTICLES RELATED TO LAW (Found in non-law journals), Oceana

LEGAL PERIODICAL DIGEST, C.C.H.

G. **Political science**

1. Political Science

a. *Guides to study and dictionaries*

Brock, Clifton, THE LITERATURE OF POLITICAL SCIENCE: A GUIDE FOR STUDENTS,

Bowker, 1969

Dunner, J. (ed.), DICTIONARY OF POLITICAL
SCIENCE, Philosophical, 1964

Merritt, R.L. and Pyszka, G.J., THE STUDENT
POLITICAL SCIENTIST'S HANDBOOK,
Schenkman, 1969

Roberts, G.K., A DICTIONARY OF POLITICAL
ANALYSIS, St. Martin's, 1971

Sperber, H. and Trittschuh, T., AMERICAN
POLITICAL TERMS: AN HISTORICAL DIC-
TIONARY, Wayne State, 1962

b. Handbooks and encyclopedias

Normandin, G.P. (ed.), CANADIAN PARLIA-
MENTARY GUIDE, Syndicat Des Oeuvres
Sociales Ltd.

BOOK OF THE STATES (BIENNIAL) (Handbook
of U.S. States), Council of State Gov-
ernments, Chicago

CANADA YEARBOOK

MUNICIPAL YEARBOOK (Annual, Handbook
of U.S. Cities), International City Mana-
gers Assn., Chicago

c. Indexes

ABC POL. SCI. ADVANCED BIBLIOGRAPHY OF
CONTENTS: POLITICAL SCIENCE AND GOV-
ERNMENT (Political Science Index), ABC-
CLIO Santa Barbara, Calif.

CANADIAN GOVT. PUBLICATIONS CATALOGUE
MONTHLY

INTERNATIONAL POLITICAL SCIENCE
ABSTRACTS

MONTHLY CATALOG OF UNITED STATES GOV-
ERNMENT PUBLICATIONS

PUBLIC ADMINISTRATION REVIEW

SAGE PUBLIC ADMINISTRATION ABSTRACTS,
Sage Pub.

2. International Affairs

   a. Guides to study and dictionaries

      Brimmer, B. et al., A GUIDE TO THE USE OF UNITED NATIONS DOCUMENTS, Oceana, 1962

   b. Handbooks and encyclopedias

      Institute of Electoral Research, London, PARLIAMENTS AND ELECTORAL SYSTEMS, A WORLD HANDBOOK, I.E.R., 1962

      Kernig, G.D. (ed.), MARXISM, COMMUNISM AND WESTERN SOCIETY: A COMPARATIVE ENCYCLOPEDIA, Herder & Herder, 1972

      Palmer, M. et al., POLITICAL AND ECONOMIC PLANNING, A HANDBOOK OF EUROPEAN ORGANIZATIONS, Michael, 1968

      Vincent, J.E., A HANDBOOK OF INTERNATIONAL RELATIONS: A GUIDE TO TERMS, THEORY AND PRACTICE, Woodbury, 1969

      Vincent, J.E., A HANDBOOK OF THE UNITED NATIONS, Woodbury, 1969

      ANNUAL REGISTER OF WORLD EVENTS

      FACTS ON FILE (Weekly World News Digest)

      POLITICAL HANDBOOK AND ATLAS OF THE WORLD (ANNUAL)

      UNITED STATES IN WORLD AFFAIRS (ANNUAL), Council on Foreign Relations

      YEARBOOK OF WORLD AFFAIRS

      YEARBOOK OF THE UNITED NATIONS

   c. Indexes

      UNITED NATIONS DOCUMENTS INDEX

      PEACE RESEARCH ABSTRACTS

H. Psychology

   a. Guides to study and dictionaries

      Bell, J.E., A GUIDE TO LIBRARY RESEARCH IN PSYCHOLOGY, 1971

      Brussel, J.A., and Cantzlaar, G., THE LAYMAN'S DICTIONARY OF PSYCHIATRY, 1967

Drever, J., A DICTIONARY OF PSYCHOLOGY (rev. ed.), Penguin, 1964

Wolman, B.B., DICTIONARY OF BEHAVIOURAL SCIENCE, Van Nostrand, 1974

b. *Handbooks and encyclopedias*

Arieti, S. (ed.), AMERICAN HANDBOOK OF PSYCHIATRY, 1966

Borgatta, E.F. and Lambert, W.W., HANDBOOK OF PERSONALITY THEORY AND RESEARCH, Rand McNally, 1968

Deutsch, A. (ed.), ENCYCLOPEDIA OF MENTAL HEALTH, Watts, 1963

Eidelberg, L., ENCYCLOPEDIA OF PSYCHOANALYSIS, Free Press, 1968

Eysenck, Arnold and Meili (ed.), ENCYCLOPEDIA OF PSYCHOLOGY, Herder and Herder, 1972

Goldenson, R.M., THE ENCYCLOPEDIA OF HUMAN BEHAVIOUR, PSYCHOLOGY, PSYCHIATRY, AND MENTAL HEALTH, Doubleday, 1968

Gruenberg, S.M., ENCYCLOPEDIA OF CHILD CARE AND GUIDANCE, Doubleday, 1963

Harriman, P.L., HANDBOOK OF PSYCHOLOGICAL TERMS, Littlefield, Adams, 1965

Lindzey, G. (ed.), HANDBOOK OF SOCIAL PSYCHOLOGY, (2nd ed.), Addison-Wesley, 1968

Stevens, S.S., HANDBOOK OF EXPERIMENTAL PSYCHOLOGY, Wiley, 1951

Wolman, B.B. (ed.), HANDBOOK OF CLINICAL PSYCHOLOGY, McGraw-Hill, 1965

Wolman, B.B. (ed.), HANDBOOK OF GENERAL PSYCHIATRY, Prentice-Hall, 1973

ANNUAL REVIEW OF PSYCHOLOGY

MENTAL RETARDATION (ANNUAL REVIEW)

c. *Indexes*

CHILD DEVELOPMENT ABSTRACTS AND BIB-

LIOGRAPHY
LITERATURE AND PSYCHOLOGY BIBLIOG-
RAPHY
PSYCHOLOGICAL ABSTRACTS
PSYCHOPHARMACOLOGY ABSTRACTS

I. **Sociology**

a. Guides to study and dictionaries

Davis, J.P. (ed.), THE AMERICAN NEGRO REF-
ERENCE BOOK, Prentice-Hall, 1966

Fairchild, H.P., DICTIONARY OF SOCIOLOGY,
Littlefield, Adams, 1970

Mitchell, G.D., A DICTIONARY OF SOCIOLOGY,
Aldine, 1968

Theodorson, G.A. & Theodorson, A.G.,
MODERN DICTIONARY OF SOCIOLOGY,
Crowell, 1969

Wheeler, H., WOMANHOOD MEDIA: CURRENT
RESOURCES ABOUT WOMEN, 1972

Young, E.F., DICTIONARY OF SOCIAL WEL-
FARE, Social Sciences Pub., 1948

b. Handbooks and encyclopedias

Branham, V. and Kutash, S., ENCYCLOPEDIA
OF CRIMINOLOGY, Philosophical, 1949.

Christensen, H.T. (ed.), HANDBOOK OF MAR-
RIAGE AND THE FAMILY, Rand McNally,
1964

Farris, R.E.L. (ed.), HANDBOOK OF MODERN
SOCIOLOGY, Rand McNally, 1964

Goslin, D.A. (ed.), HANDBOOK SOCIALIZA-
TION THEORY AND RESEARCH, Rand Mc-
Nally, 1969

Lindzey, G. (ed.), HANDBOOK OF SOCIAL
PSYCHOLOGY, Addison-Wesley

March, J.G. (ed.), HANDBOOK OF ORGANIZA-
TIONS, Rand McNally, 1964

ENCYCLOPEDIA OF SOCIAL WORK (Successor to
the social work year book), Nat. Assoc. of
Social Workers, 1971

WOMEN'S WORK AND WOMEN'S STUDIES AN-
NUAL, N.Y. Women's Center, Barnard
College, 1972
c. Indexes
BLACK INFORMATION INDEX, Infonetics
DRUG ABUSE BIBLIOGRAPHY (ANNUAL),
Whitson
SOCIOLOGICAL ABSTRACTS
ABSTRACTS FOR SOCIAL WORKERS, National
Assn. of Social Workers
WOMEN STUDIES ABSTRACTS

IV. URBAN AND ENVIRONMENTAL STUDIES
A. Urban studies (Planning and architecture)
a. Guides to study and dictionaries
Abrams, C., THE LANGUAGE OF CITIES, Vik-
ing, 1971
Phillips, M., GUIDE TO ARCHITECTURAL IN-
FORMATION, Design Data Center, 1971
Saylor, H.H., DICTIONARY OF ARCHITEC-
TURE, Wiley, 1952
b. Handbooks and encyclopedias
Amer. Instit. of Architects, HANDBOOK OF
ARCHITECTURAL PRACTICE, AIA, 1958
Hatje, G., ENCYCLOPEDIA OF MODERN AR-
CHITECTURE, Thames & Hudson, 1963
Hauser, P.M., HANDBOOK FOR SOCIAL RE-
SEARCH IN URBAN AREAS, UNESCO, 1965
Whittick, A. (ed.), ENCYCLOPEDIA OF URBAN
PLANNING, McGraw-Hill, 1974
QUARTERLY DIGEST OF URBAN AND REGIONAL
RESEARCH, Univ. of Illinois
c. Indexes
Bell & Roeder, URBAN ENVIRONMENTS AND
HUMAN BEHAVIOR: AN ANNOTATED BIB-
LIOGRAPHY, Dowden, Hutchinson & Ross,
1973
Branch, M.C., COMPREHENSIVE URBAN
PLANNING: A SELECTIVE ANNOTATED BIB-

LIOGRAPHY, Sage, 1970

Canadian Council of Urban and Regional Research, URBAN CANADA, (formerly URBAN AND REGIONAL REFERENCES)

Columbia Univ., AVERY INDEX TO ARCHITECTURAL PERIODICALS, G.K. Hall

Council of Planning Librarians, INDEX TO CITY PLANNING LIBRARIES EXCHANGE BIBLIOGRAPHIES, C.P.L., 1974

U.S. Dept. H.U.D., NEW COMMUNITIES: A BIBLIOGRAPHY. U.S.G.P.O., 1970

B. **Environmental studies**

a. *Guides to study and dictionaries*

Hanson, H.C., DICTIONARY OF ECOLOGY, Owen, 1962

Veatch, J.O., WATER AND WATER USE TERMINOLOGY, Thomas, 1966

b. *Handbooks and encyclopedias*

Amer. Public Health Assoc., GUIDE TO THE APPRAISAL AND CONTROL OF AIR POLLUTION, A.P.H.A., 1969

Dept. of Environment, Inland Waters (Canada), CANADA WATER YEARBOOK

ECO/LOG Information Service, CANADIAN POLLUTION LEGISLATION, Chinook Chemicals

Lund, H.F., INDUSTRIAL POLLUTION CONTROL HANDBOOK, McGraw-Hill, 1971

Sarnoff, P., THE NEW YORK TIMES ENCYCLOPEDIC DICTIONARY OF THE ENVIRONMENT, Quadrangle, 1971

Todd, D.F. (ed.), THE WATER ENCYCLOPEDIA, Water Info. Centre, 1970

Van Der Leeden, F., WATER RESOURCES OF THE WORLD, Water Info. Centre, 1975

CRC HANDBOOK OF ENVIRONMENTAL CONTROL, CRC Press

a. *Guides to study and dictionaries*

Blanchard & Ostvold, LITERATURE OF AG-
RICULTURAL RESEARCH. Univ. of Calif.,
1958

Bottle & Wyatt, THE USE OF BIOLOGICAL
LITERATURE, Archon Books, 1971

Gray, P., THE DICTIONARY OF THE BIOLOGI-
CAL SCIENCES, Reinhold, 1967

King, C., A DICTIONARY OF GENETICS, Oxford, 1974

Pennak, R.W., COLLEGIATE DICTIONARY OF
ZOOLOGY, Ronald, 1964

Smith & Reid, GUIDE TO LITERATURE OF THE
LIFE SCIENCES (8th ed.) Burgess, 1972

b. *Handbooks and encyclopedias*

Altman & Dittmer, BIOLOGY DATA BOOK,
F.A.S.E.B., 1974

Fisher & Vincent, WILDLIFE IN DANGER,
Viking, 1969

Gray, P., THE ENCYCLOPEDIA OF THE BIOLOG-
ICAL SCIENCES (2nd ed.), Van Nostrand
Reinhold, 1970

Grzimek, B. (ed.), GRZIMEK'S ANIMAL LIFE
ENCYCLOPEDIA, Van Nostrand Reinhold,
1972

Miller & West, ENCYCLOPEDIA OF ANIMAL
CARE, Williams & Wilkins, 1972

Siegmund (ed.), MERCK VETERINARY MAN-
UAL: A HANDBOOK OF DIAGNOSIS AND
THERAPY, Merck, 1967

c. *Indexes*

AGRICULTURAL INDEX

BIOLOGICAL ABSTRACTS

BIOLOGICAL & AGRICULTURAL INDEX

CATALOG OF MEDICAL AND VETERINARY
ZOOLOGY

WILDLIFE ABSTRACTS

C. **Chemistry**
   a. *Guides to study and dictionaries*
   Bottle, R.T., THE USE OF CHEMICAL LITERA-
   TURE, Archon Books, 1969
   Crane, Austin & Marr, A GUIDE TO THE
   LITERATURE OF CHEMISTRY, Wiley, 1957
   Flood, W.E., THE DICTIONARY OF CHEMICAL
   NAMES, Philosophical, 1963
   Hawley, G.G., THE CONDENSED CHEMICAL
   DICTIONARY (8th ed.), Van Nostrand
   Reinhold, 1971
   Snell & Snell, DICTIONARY OF COMMERCIAL
   CHEMICALS, Van Nostrand, 1962
   b. *Handbooks and encyclopedias*
   Hampel & Hawley (ed.), THE ENCYCLOPEDIA
   OF CHEMISTRY, Van Nostrand Reinhold,
   1973
   Lang, N.A., LANG'S HANDBOOK OF CHEMIS-
   TRY (11th ed.), McGraw-Hill, 1973
   Stecher (ed.), MERCK INDEX: AN ENCYC-
   LOPEDIA OF CHEMICALS AND DRUGS,
   Merck, 1968
   c. *Indexes*
   CHEMICAL ABSTRACTS
D. **Earth sciences** (geology, oceanography, hyd-
   rology, meterology)
   a. *Guides to study and dictionaries*
   Challinor, J., A DICTIONARY OF GEOLOGY,
   Oxford, 1974
   Gary et al., (ed.), GLOSSARY OF GEOLOGY,
   Amer. Geol. Instit., 1972
   Hunt & Groves, A GLOSSARY OF OCEAN
   SCIENCE AND UNDERSEA TECHNOLOGY
   TERMS, Compass, 1965
   Huschke, R.E. (ed.), GLOSSARY OF
   METEOROLOGY, Amer. Met. Soc., 1959
   Kaplan, R., A GUIDE TO INFORMATION
   SOURCES IN MINING, MINERALS, AND GEOS-

CIENCES, Interscience, 1965

Runcorn et al., INTERNATIONAL DICTIONARY OF GEOPHYSICS, SEISMOLOGY, GEOMAGNETISM, AERONOMY, OCEANOGRAPHY, GEODESY, GRAVITY, MARINE GEOPHYSICS, METEOROLOGY, THE EARTH AS A PLANET AND ITS EVOLUTION, Pergamon, 1967

Thrush, P.W., A DICTIONARY OF MINING, MINERALS AND RELATED TERMS, U.S. Bureau of Mines, 1968

Ward & Wheeler, GEOLOGIC REFERENCE SOURCES, Scarecrow, 1972

Wood, D.N., USE OF EARTH SCIENCES LITERATURE, Archon Books, 1973

b. Handbooks and encyclopedias

Bogel, H., A COLLECTOR'S GUIDE TO MINERALS AND GEMSTONES, Thames & Hudson, 1971

Chow, V.T., HANDBOOK OF APPLIED HYDROLOGY, McGraw-Hill, 1964

Dept. of Energy, Mines & Resources (Canada), CANADIAN MINERALS YEARBOOK

Fairbridge, R.W., THE ENCYCLOPEDIA OF WORLD REGIONAL GEOLOGY, Dowden, Hutchinson, Ross, 1975

Fenton & Fenton, THE FOSSIL BOOK, Doubleday, 1958

Firth, F.E. (ed.), THE ENCYCLOPEDIA OF MARINE RESOURCES, Van Nostrand Reinhold, 1969

Malone, T.F. (ed.), COMPENDIUM OF METEOROLOGY, Amer. Met. Soc., 1951

Pough, F.H., A FIELD GUIDE TO ROCKS AND MINERALS, Houghton, 1960

U.S. Bureau of Mines, MINERALS YEARBOOK

U.S. Coast & Geodetic Survey, EARTHQUAKE HISTORY OF THE U.S., 1966

U.S. Environmental Data Service, WORLD

WEATHER RECORDS

ENCYCLOPEDIA OF EARTH SCIENCES

c. Indexes

ABSTRACTS OF NORTH AMERICAN GEOLOGY

BIBLIOGRAPHY AND INDEX OF GEOLOGY

CHEMICAL ABSTRACTS

METEOROLOGY AND GEOASTROPHYSICAL ABSTRACTS

OCEAN ABSTRACTS

E. **Physics and mathematics** (astronomy, space and engineering)

a. Guides to study and dictionaries

Dick, M., CURRENT INFORMATION SOURCES IN MATHEMATICS, Libraries Unlimited, 1973

Engineers Joint Council, THESAURUS OF ENGINEERING AND SCIENTIFIC TERMS, E.J.C., 1967

Freiberger, W.F. (ed.), INTERNATIONAL DICTIONARY OF APPLIED MATHEMATICS, Van Nostrand, 1960

Glenn & James, MATHEMATICS DICTIONARY, Van Nostrand, 1968

Parke, N.G., GUIDE TO THE LITERATURE OF MATHEMATICS AND PHYSICS INCLUDING RELATED WORKS ON ENGINEERING SCIENCE, Dover, 1958

Parsons, S.A.J., HOW TO FIND OUT ABOUT ENGINEERING, Pergamon, 1972

Thewlis, J., CONCISE DICTIONARY OF PHYSICS AND RELATED SUBJECTS, Pergamon, 1973

Whitford, R.H., PHYSICS LITERATURE: A REFERENCE MANUAL, Scarecrow, 1968

b. Handbooks of encyclopedias

Besàncon, R.M., THE ENCYCLOPEDIA OF PHYSICS, Van Nostrand Reinhold, 1974

Billings, B.H. (ed.), AMERICAN INSTITUTE OF PHYSICS HANDBOOK, McGraw-Hill, 1972

Bizony, M.T. (ed.), THE NEW SPACE ENCYC-
LOPEDIA: A GUIDE TO ASTRONOMY AND
SPACE EXPLORATION, Dutton, 1973

Eshbach, O.W., HANDBOOK OF ENGINEERING
FUNDAMENTALS, Wiley, 1952

Jones & Schubert (eds.), ENGINEERING EN-
CYCLOPEDIA, Industrial Press, 1963

Muller, P., CONCISE ENCYCLOPEDIA OF AS-
TRONOMY, Follett, 1968

Potter, J.H. (ed.), HANDBOOK OF THE EN-
GINEERING SCIENCES, Van Nostrand, 1967

Urquhart, L.C., CIVIL ENGINEERING HAND-
BOOK, McGraw-Hill, 1959

UNIVERSAL ENCYCLOPEDIA OF MATHEMATICS,
Simon & Schuster, 1964

c. Indexes

Kemp, D.A., ASTRONOMY AND AS-
TROPHYSICS, Archon Books, 1970

ENGINEERING ABSTRACTS

ENGINEERING INDEX

MATHEMATICAL REVIEW

PHYSICS ABSTRACTS

F. **Medical sciences**

a. Guides to study and dictionaries

Amer. Hospital Assn., THE AHA GUIDE TO
THE HEALTH CARE FIELD, A.H.A. (annual)

Amer. Medical Assn., CURRENT MEDICAL
INFORMATION AND TERMINOLOGY,
A.M.A., 1971

Bander & Wallach, MEDICAL LEGAL DICTIO-
NARY, Oceana, 1970

Bender, A.E., DICTIONARY OF NUTRITION
AND FOOD TECHNOLOGY, Butterworth,
1965

Boucher, C.O. (ed.), CURRENT CLINICAL DE-
NTAL TERMINOLOGY, Mosby, 1974

Magalini, S., DICTIONARY OF MEDICAL SYN-
DROMES, Lippincott, 1971

b. *Handbooks and encyclopedias*

Deichmann & Gerards, TOXICOLOGY OF DRUGS AND CHEMICALS, Academic, 1969

Grad, F.P., PUBLIC HEALTH LAW MANUAL: A HANDBOOK ON THE LEGAL ASPECTS OF PUBLIC HEALTH ADMINISTRATION AND ENFORCEMENT, A.P.H.A., 1970

Hansen, H.F., ENCYCLOPEDIC GUIDE TO NURSING, McGraw-Hill, 1957

Kaye, S., HANDBOOK OF EMERGENCY TOXICOLOGY, Thomas, 1970

McElroy & Malone, HANDBOOK OF ORAL DIAGNOSIS AND TREATMENT PLANNING, Williams & Wilkins, 1969

Miller & Keane, ENCYCLOPEDIA AND DICTIONARY OF MEDICINE AND NURSING, Saunders, 1972

Parr & Young (eds.), PARR'S CONCISE MEDICAL ENCYCLOPEDIA, Elsevier, 1965

Shartel & Plant, THE LAW OF MEDICAL PRACTICE, Thomas, 1959

Sunshine, I. (ed.), HANDBOOK OF ANALYTICAL TOXICOLOGY, C.C.R.C., 1969

THE PHARMACOPOEIA OF THE U.S.A., Merck

UNLISTED DRUGS (list of new drugs not in Pharmacopoeia)

c. *Indexes*

Black, A.D., INDEX OF THE PERIODICAL DENTAL LITERATURE

Nick, W.V., INDEX OF LEGAL MEDICINE, Legal Medicine Press

ABSTRACTS ON HYGIENE

AMERICAN DRUG INDEX

CUMULATIVE INDEX TO NURSING LITERATURE

DENTAL ABSTRACTS

INDEX MEDICUS

INTERNATIONAL NURSING INDEX

ORAL RESEARCH ABSTRACTS (Dentistry)

Printed in Canada